HERE
I AM

RenewedMinds

HERE
I AM

NOW WHAT ON EARTH
SHOULD I BE DOING?

QUENTIN J.
SCHULTZE

A RenewedMinds Book

BakerBooks
Grand Rapids, Michigan

To
Harvey and Annie Gainey
for helping so many young people
discover the greatest calling

© 2005 by Quentin J. Schultze

Published by Baker Books
a division of Baker Publishing Group
P.O. Box 6287, Grand Rapids, MI 49516-6287
www.bakerbooks.com

Printed in the United States of America

Library of Congress Cataloging-in-Publication Data
Schultze, Quentin J. (Quentin James), 1952-
    Here I am : now what on earth should I be doing? / Quentin J. Schultze.
        p.   cm.
    Includes bibliographical references.
    ISBN 10: 0-8010-6545-3 (pbk.)
    ISBN 978-0-8010-6545-3 (pbk.)
    1. Vocation—Christianity. 2. Christian life. I. Title.
    BV4740.S33 2005
    248.4—dc22   2004024201

Contents

133807

Acknowledgments

I owe the most to God's Word, the greatest source of wisdom about vocation.

I am also indebted to many Hebrews and Christians who have interpreted that Word faithfully. I have borrowed special insights from Saints Augustine of Hippo and Francis of Assisi, Rabbi Abraham Heschel, Reformers John Calvin and Martin Luther, and contemporary writers from Thomas Merton to Dietrich Bonhoeffer. I summarize key sources at the back of the book.

Students in my Senior Seminar in Communication class at Calvin College charitably critiqued the manuscript: Eric S. Evenhouse, Art Bamford, Brendan Wright, David Neal Boomker, Emily Huck, Davis C. Watson, Melanie De Nooy, Katherine Sikma, Cat Hoort, Jessica L. Vande Vusse, Ashley Payne, Becky Sletto, Lisa Ryckbost, Lisa Van Grouw, Jacob M. Wilkoff, Julie Heerema, Anne Plasman, and Derek DeWeerd.

Other friends and former students who gave me excellent advice are Gloria F. Jea, Sara Jane Toering, Brad Van Arragon, Tom Schwanda, Ren Broekhuizen, and Judi DeJager.

I owe a special debt to a number of Calvin College colleagues, including Glen VanAndel, Kevin Dougherty, Steve VanderLeest, Wayne Wentzheimer, and Hessel Bouma III.

Friends at other institutions also read the manuscript, sometimes with their students: Tom Ribar of Waynesburg College; Paul Butler of Moody Bible Institute; Tom Jones of Taylor University; Margaret Stowell Wheeler of Cedarville University; Susan L. and Gerald J. Bisecker-Mast, Dan Fultz, and Hans Houshower of Bluffton College; Timothy Detwiler of Cornerstone University; Nelvin Vos of Muhlenburg College; and Darwin Glassford of Montreat College.

Bob Hosack and Stephanie Vink served me with joy and expertise as editors. Paula Gibson steered the graphic design with vision and creativity.

The Lilly Vocation Project at Calvin College, funded by the Lilly Endowment, Inc., awarded two grants that enabled me to write this book. I am grateful for the insights of project associates Shirley Roels, Ron Rienstra, Ed Seely, Claudia Beversluis, Laura Smit, Dale Cooper, Paul Ryan, Cindy de Jong, Shirley Hoogstra, Beth Kok, and Miriam Ippel.

Barbara Schultze counseled me wisely, as always.

My parents, Theodore and Agnes, blessed me in ways that they probably never recognized. God used even their weaknesses to nurture my faith and direct my life.

Meanwhile, "Here I am, Lord."

Introduction

During thirty years of teaching and mentoring, I have repeatedly witnessed how God calls, equips, challenges, and blesses faithful followers. Nearly every day I hear from former students who are celebrating a new job or promotion, tackling a difficult ethical dilemma, praising God for a spouse or child, or lamenting poor professional and personal decisions.

I began thinking seriously about God's call during my college years. As I explain in this book, the result has been a professional and personal adventure.

According to the biblical pattern, God calls people like you and me to participate in eternal plans. He wants us to reply faithfully. When we do, we discover that God employs both our strengths and our weaknesses in the "renewing of all things."

Scripture and life experience both demonstrate that God calls us on two levels. One is the *vocation* shared by all followers of Jesus Christ. The Bible says that each of us is called to care for God's world. The Old Testament defines this caring as "being a blessing to others." The New Testament focuses on "loving God and neighbor." God calls his people of all ages to be sacrificial care-*takers*, not to selfish career-*seekers*.

The other level of calling includes each person's many *stations*—the particular places, relationships, and work in and through which a person cares. For instance, our jobs, hobbies, and families provide stations. We might care as parents, siblings, church members, and employees. Although our overall vocation as caretakers never changes, many of our stations do—nearly every day. God wants us to respond favorably to our shared vocation and to our own stations so that we might flourish in community, serving others as they serve us.

Our calling is a lifelong process of connecting our shared vocation with our individual stations. As Scripture puts it, we are called to "work out" our faith just as God works in us.[1] In short, throughout life we need to ask ourselves how to apply our faith to our stations. Answering that question faithfully is the daily adventure in vocational living.

Throughout this book I use biblical examples, my own experiences, and others' life stories to show how God calls, challenges, and ultimately blesses faithful followers during their vocational journeys. Frequently this adventure is confusing and even discouraging, but our overall calling remains the same throughout.

The Lord calls. We should listen and obey. Whenever we do, we choose life. Whenever we don't, we choose death. In either case, our own lives become contemporary parables. As my aunt Kay used to say, "That's my story, and I'm stuck with it."

1

Listening to God

God calls Abraham to travel three days to Mount Moriah, where he is supposed to sacrifice his only son, Isaac. Abraham obeys, but at the last moment, God's messenger intervenes, saving Isaac.

Abraham's incredible experience captures the way God calls all of us in the midst of our own fears and doubts. Like Abraham, we don't know in advance what God will ask us to do. Nevertheless, we are called to sacrifice our talents and resources even for such uncertain tasks. Much of the world would call this foolishness.

Yet the Bible describes a personal God who calls followers to become living sacrifices. *Vocation* comes from the Latin *vocatio*, which means "voice calling" or simply "calling." Throughout the Scriptures, God's "voice" engages people, interrupting their own agendas and directing them to become faithful followers.

This is all a splendid mystery. We cannot know our particular futures, but like Abraham, we do know that God wants us to be a blessing to others. Abraham obediently travels to Moriah, probably wondering about God's plans. How could he be a great blessing to future generations if his only son is sacrificed? Abraham was probably baffled by, and yet excited about, the possibility that God would give him offspring more numerous than the stars in the skies.

Like Abraham, we face doubts and challenges as we follow God in faith. Uncertainty is part of the vocational adventure. Throughout life, we all will say, "I never imagined. . . ." But God did. No one is more creative, more surprising, more involved in our lives than the Lord.

There is no single calling, one-track plan, or changeless career for our lives. Even Abraham's trip to Moriah was just one episode in a life of uncanny ups and downs as well as surprising twists and turns. He was not called merely to a job, profession, or occupation. Abraham was called to obedience, to worship God in every part of his life, from hospitality to marriage to sacrificing his son.

We are called to follow Jesus Christ. This is our overarching vocation. But we are also called to follow Jesus into many different "stations," serving perhaps as parents, workers, church members, civic leaders, neighbors, and far more. God wants us to follow him faithfully into every area of our lives, thereby becoming living sacrifices who care responsibly for God's world.

Knowing That God Calls

Often we do our best to discern God's calls. We pray feverishly, take personality inventories, and seek professional as well as personal advice. Still, no calls arrive directly from God. Scripture teaches that God calls, but we imperfect creatures still struggle to know how, when, and where to serve God. As followers of Jesus Christ, we live by faith.[1] So we go on in faith.

My father, a Chicago cab driver, loved to tell the story of a passenger he picked up early one morning. As his taxi rolled to a stop in front of an apartment building, a woman ran up to the vehicle, opened a rear door, and hopped into the seat. "Where to?" my father asked.

"Get going! I'll tell you when we get there!" she exclaimed.

Often our approach to calling is like this passenger's overly eager desire to get going. We impatiently want to forge ahead to an unclear destination instead of taking the time to learn how to be faithful.

The mystery of vocation is more like an unfolding relationship than a carefully planned trip. As we come to know God better and to know ourselves in relationship to God, we also discern where and how to serve—but rarely with absolute certainty.

One of my students came from a family of teachers, but he was sure that teaching was the one profession that didn't suit him. He considered filmmaking or music. Then he began feeling called to become a college teacher, so he applied for graduate school. Dismayed when the university he wanted to attend turned him down, he humbly prayed to God for help.

Shortly thereafter, he visited a different graduate program at the same university and within minutes was admitted and then assigned courses to teach. His life was turned upside-down twice in a matter of hours. Now he wonders if God used the initial graduate-school rejection to remind him to depend on the Lord. In any case, he rightly realizes that occupational callings emerge out of a faithful relationship *with* God, not just a message *from* God.

When we become Jesus's followers and join a community of believers, we are best equipped to discern our strengths and weaknesses and to learn about opportunities to serve. Listening to others' stories of vocation helps us to discover our own callings. We then see that faithfulness is partly accepting the mystery of how God works through followers' ups and downs, baffling turnarounds, failures, and fresh starts.

A former student of mine in Michigan drove 1,700 miles to the West Coast partly because he liked the weather there. The second day in a city where he knew hardly anyone, he was sightseeing downtown and happened across the office building of a company he recognized from his online research. He boldly went inside and asked if they were hiring, and before long he had a fine position with that small but rapidly growing company. He thrived on the challenging work, the long hours, the rigorous deadlines, being a Christian witness through his work, and meeting clients from around the globe.

Later he left the firm to accept a promising position with a new company, which soon went bankrupt. He went to graduate school for his M.B.A. Here's a summary of his unfolding story: impressive college record, great job, notable success, upward mobility, fine marriage, risky career change, business failure, time to think and pray, grad school. What's next for him? I'm looking forward to finding out. So is he.

Another graduate went to Nashville absolutely convinced that God wanted her to serve in the Christian music business. She was the kind of person I would hire: industrious, articulate, hardworking, and faithful. Plus, she knew Christian music. She moved to the music city in faith. From what I could tell, she did everything right to find a position.

After many months, however, she gave up and settled gratefully for a job in a different field. She's still baffled about her earlier sense of occupational calling. Was she wrong about God's will? Was she too early on the music trail?

In spite of our confusion about callings, God claims us for service before we are aware of it. "All the days ordained for me were written in your book before one of them came to be," proclaims the psalmist.[2] God "chose" us in Jesus Christ, Paul writes.[3] I don't pretend to comprehend this.

In spite of such comforting words, however, we ought not to wait around for perfect knowledge of God's plans for us. Recently a man guiltily told me in private that he wasn't sure about God's calling. "Neither am I," I admitted. But I added that we must go on, being faithful followers wherever our journey takes us.

Faith is patient, not lazy. The great Christian writer John Milton (1608–1674) wrote after he had gone blind, "They also serve who only stand and wait." Following Christ is an ongoing journey, not a one-time blast of revelation or a straight trajectory.

Nevertheless, God's calls sometimes are too crystal clear to ignore, although even obvious occupational calls usually lead us to a general field of work rather than to particular jobs or tasks.

Before his conversion to Christ, Saul (later called Paul) believed that his purpose in life was to discredit Jesus and his followers. Saul became a professional critic. He had a gift! Then Saul journeyed toward Damascus, where God called him to become a preaching follower. The people traveling with Saul were speechless.[4] After all, Saul probably was among those least likely to follow Jesus.

As the book of Acts and Paul's letters demonstrate, he spent the rest of his life trying to figure out how to be a *follower* (one who is called). For him, vocation led to traveling as a missionary, preaching here and there, encouraging other believers, spending time in prison, escaping from hostile crowds, advising churches on how to settle staff and theological conflicts, and recruiting more followers. In these and other ways, he cared for the emerging church of Jesus Christ. All such activities became his many *stations*.

Identifying Our *Vocation* and *Stations*

We can partly solve the mystery of God's callings by distinguishing between our shared vocation and each person's particular stations. *Our vocation is to be caring followers of Jesus Christ who faithfully love God, neighbor, and self.*[5]

God calls each of us to this overall task of caring for his world. In a broad sense, this caretaking is our vocation as Jesus Christ's ambassadors on earth.

Even after hearing the overarching call, however, we still have to discern how to care faithfully in specific contexts, such as sharing the gospel with a friend, comforting a co-worker, running a business profitably, and serving patients or clients.

Our stations *include our jobs, situations, and relationships.* A few stations are definable roles, such as manager, parent, student, nurse, and deacon. Others are too informal to identify precisely—such as caring for a lost child or listening empathically to a suffering co-worker who is struggling to save a failing marriage.

God calls us to both our shared vocation and the various stations where we can "work out" our faith concretely.[6] He provides stations so we can all serve each other for the good of society as well as church. Each of us depends on other stations, such as parent, doctor, engineer, and teacher. The number of people and stations involved in designing, manufacturing, marketing, selling, and repairing the car I drive is mind-boggling.

The historical meaning of station is "where one keeps watch," like a sentry, guard, or overseer.[7] In our stations, we caretakers stand watch on behalf of the Lord in the service of others. As a next-door neighbor, I watch out for the kids playing in the street. As a college instructor, I monitor my teaching and students' learning. As a cook at home, I prepare meals for my family when it's

my turn. I ensure that the wash is clean and the lawn is watered.
I also stay on the lookout along with my wife for ways that we
can help the needy in our church, community, and nation. We
listen, learn, and follow the leading of the Spirit.

None of us can determine from the Bible precisely which stations to pursue. Most of our stations emerge as we pay attention
to the needs and opportunities that present themselves. Someone
asks us to help out at church. We discover that we are falling in
love. We enjoy a college course so much that we decide to major
in that field. Every one of our job applications is rejected except
for one—which leads to an offer that we decide to accept. We
lose our job or suffer illness.

Access to many stations is partly a matter of social privilege. A
college education is an advantage denied to many North Ameri-
cans and to most of the world's population. So are internships
and job training. In some countries, even worshipping publicly is
a privilege. Because social factors limit as well as open up access
to stations, each of us is born into particular opportunities and
limitations. The most just societies provide adequate freedom
and opportunity, but no society is perfect. Although some people
are blessed with manifold opportunities, most of us have to face
the realities of global, local, and personal circumstances that
greatly limit our choices. Flexibility is essential.

Some theologians argued centuries ago that God gives each
human being one lifelong work station in order to keep him or
her from being lazy and unproductive. Perhaps such was the
case then, but today jobs come and go. People win and lose
promotions. Layoffs devastate employees' families and communities. Government regulations and international political and
monetary policies impact domestic economies. Midlife career
shifts are increasingly common. So is going back to school to
learn new skills and enter different professions. As a result, we
should remain open to the possibility of a lifetime of occupational moves, perhaps even two or three major career changes.
Flexibility and faith are critically important.

Even amidst such turbulence, however, we usually can identify our immediate stations. We might be a grandchild, friend,
accountant, mentor, volunteer, or Sunday school teacher—or
all at the same time. We might take off a year from school or
career in order to reflect and pray for guidance or volunteer for

a nonprofit agency. Such a respite can be a time for new learning and special serving. It might be particularly appropriate when the job market doesn't match our occupational goals. God blesses us with temporary stations even when we are uncertain about the long run.

We are called to connect our shared vocation of caretaking to our own, changing stations. In doing so, we work out our faith in every area of life.

Responding in Faith

Since God does call us to follow him in all stations, we ought to respond faithfully. The angel tells Mary that she will serve as the mother of Jesus Christ. Mary offers one of the greatest responses to God's call: "May it be to me as you have said."[8]

This was a staggering, humble response to an unfathomable event. Mary was a young girl, probably about thirteen years old, pregnant and undoubtedly baffled. From a purely earthly perspective, the whole episode was outlandish. God comes to a peasant girl on the bottom of the social ladder? Her reputation was on the line—and surely telling others that God conceived her child would not solve her problem! Worse yet, Joseph might abandon her in disgrace. If so, she faced certain poverty and probably a life of public ridicule and private gossip.

But God does call people in ways that defy human understanding. God advises Noah to build an ark, fill it with animals and family, and set sail. Jesus calls fishermen to follow him. The Lord invites Thomas to examine his crucifixion wounds in the upper room. In spite of their doubts, these saints, like Mary, respond in faith.

Biblical examples might seem unrealistic because we have not personally heard God's literal voice. But the Bible is filled with illustrations of how God calls followers through ordinary as well as unique circumstances. Was John called to Patmos, the remote island where he wrote Revelation? Was Joseph called, through his brothers' evil deeds, to descend into the pit? Was King David called to write psalms? Yes to all, but not as clearly as Abraham and Mary were called.

God's callings have always been incredibly diverse and often rather ambiguous even in hindsight. We might sense a call while conversing with a friend, watching a sunset at the beach, listening to the lyrics of an inspiring song, meditating on a sermon, reading Scripture, or sitting in solitude. There is no formula. God can work through anything or anyone to call us to both vocation and stations.

Most remarkable of all, God might use our rash decisions to accomplish something far greater than we had ever imagined. I recently chatted with a successful publicist who fifteen years earlier had become an unwed mother during college. At the time she had become pregnant, she was committed to a career as a TV news anchor. But during a college-sponsored news internship, she concluded that the stress, work hours, and geographic mobility required in TV would not allow her to be a nurturing single mother. So she sought public relations work instead.

Meanwhile, she and the father of her child realized that God was calling them to marriage. They wed, finished college, and entered professions. As she recalls, the unexpected pregnancy drew her and her fiancé closer to God as well as to each other. The difficulty of raising the child on her own for a while also helped her to see the importance of seeking family-friendly employment and taught her the self-discipline she needed in later jobs.

I listened to the story of a man who had volunteered to serve in World War II. He became an Allied flight navigator and was shot down over Germany. He faced grueling marches from prison to prison, during which many soldiers died. Yet he does not doubt that by enlisting he honored God as well as served his country. In spite of the lifelong emotional effects of his time in prisons, he says that he would have made the same decision today in similar circumstances.

In the early 1900s, a teenage girl packed her bags and rode a train from her comfortable home in Asheville, North Carolina, to the mountains of Appalachia. She was prompted by hearing a preacher speak at her church about the need for teachers among the poor. This girl's daughter, Catherine Marshall, later wrote a novel, *Christy*, based on her mother's remarkable calling.

Dr. Martin Luther King Jr. accepted the call to be an increasingly influential and visible civil rights leader. Even though he received many death threats, he served in that station until his murder. King's life illustrates how the civil rights movement was guided primarily by African-Americans who learned about justice and heard calls to activism while in church.

St. Augustine (334–430) was a secular rhetorician who later accepted the call to become a minister. As a rhetorician, he had joined a profession known for selling the techniques of persuasion to anyone who could pay for them, regardless of whether the message was true or the methods of influence were noble. When Augustine became a follower of Jesus Christ as an adult, he began criticizing such unethical influence-peddling. Eventually he felt called to renew the practice of persuasion on behalf of the church. Augustine argued that since the gospel is truth, it ought to be proclaimed as convincingly as possible.

Augustine's legendary autobiography, *Confessions*, persuaded readers by revealing his past sins, his incredible conversion, and his new life in Christ. In the book, he illustrates how God called him into faith through the singing of children and his inexplicable desire to "take and read" the Bible. I doubt that he ever imagined people reading his testimony 1,600 years later in many languages. Nor could he have fathomed that his book would establish autobiography as a literary genre in the Western world. He was just learning to be a steward of the faith that God gave him.

Declaring Our Availability

We might not know with confidence which stations to pursue in God's world. But we should prepare our hearts and minds for the callings that will come. A friend wisely prays every morning, "Lord, please use me today to bless others. I'm available."

One of the richest illustrations of this declaration of availability is Abraham's response to God. God calls Abraham's name once. Abraham then declares, "Here I am."[9]

Abraham's three words, like Mary's comparable response, are worth declaring in our own lives.

Here I am. I'm not attending to my own matters. I'm ready for service.

Here *I* am. When we say "I" to God, we respond personally. We accept responsibility to listen and follow.

Here I *am*. By the grace of God, we exist—and wondrously so. As the psalmist says, we are made "a little lower than the heavenly beings" and crowned with "glory and honor."[10] We are gifted servants under God's rule. To be Jesus's followers is to become who we were created to be.

God's calls never stop. Every day presents new stations, unpredictable opportunities to praise God by being faithful followers.

Replying "Here I am" is a way of declaring our readiness, our personal responsibility, and our dependence on God. Whenever we offer these three words to God, we report for duty without knowing exactly where or how we will serve. And like Mary and Abraham, we can expect surprises along the way. Some will be great joys, others challenges.

Too often we put conditions on our availability: "Okay, Lord, since you haven't literally spoken to me, I am going to do whatever I want for a while." Putting such a demand on God is selfish.

Neither Mary nor Abraham fell back on the safety of unavailability. Their declarations of availability were affirmations of *God's* way even though they could not see the future precisely. Writer Anne Lamott says that her two favorite prayers are "Help me! Help me! Help me!" and "Thank you! Thank you! Thank you!" We could add one more: "Here I am. Use me! Use me! Use me!"

Conclusion

In this frenetic age, people tend to laugh at the idea of listening to God. But God does "call" through the Holy Spirit working in our particular circumstances.

I had no intention to go to graduate school, let alone to earn a doctoral degree—and certainly not in communication. I was a shy academic underachiever. By God's grace, however, I began focusing more on what the Lord was doing in my life than on what I wanted to accomplish. I increasingly realized—based on Scripture, prayer, worship, and conversations with friends and colleagues—that trying to control my life was foolish. In fact, I already had messed it up.

During college, I listened to friends and teachers who began asking me about attending graduate school. Then I lost my radio job. Finally, a professor urged me to apply to a doctoral program in communication. I did—and I still don't know exactly why. At least, I don't know why any more than Abraham understood how his stations would make him a blessing to people. Before long, I became a teacher.

I now realize—even though I have difficulty accepting it—that I am called with other believers to a lifelong adventure with God. The Lord is using both our trials and our accomplishments to equip us to serve others. We are God's clay.[11]

I never imagined being a teacher. Along my own mysterious journey, however, I realized that teaching fit my gifts. Somehow that occupational station chose me—which is another way of saying that God gave me the gifts and provided the opportunities to teach. I wish I had discovered this station earlier in life. But if I had, I might not have been any more faithful. I needed to prepare spiritually and emotionally. I'm still preparing—day by day as well as semester by semester. I make many mistakes. I doubt. I get upset with God. But I am still listening and trusting God to lead me on. What else can any of us do? We know how foolish it is to rely purely on our own wisdom. We do foolish things even in pursuit of God's will.

When I attended a ten-year high school reunion, some former classmates laughed when they heard that I was a professor. I chuckled too—and I still do. Why not? Sarah laughed. Abraham laughed. God called their son *Isaac* ("he laughs"). Like Mary and Paul and all believers, we are called to a frequently confusing and occasionally discouraging journey with the great "I Am." Just listen. And laugh.

2

Participating in Renewal

Recently my adult daughter decided that she was no longer going to play her drum set because she had acquired other interests. We agreed to get rid of the set since it cluttered our family room.

Initially we talked about selling the set, but we decided that we would take a few days to think about other options. We prayed for inspiration. Eventually we came up with the idea of giving the drums to a percussion student at an inner-city school.

I called the school on a Friday and told the secretary that we would like to donate the instruments to a student. She promised to explore possibilities.

The following Monday, I received a call from the school's music director. "You are not going to believe this," he said. "We were talking last week about starting a band and wondering where we would get a saxophone and drums. When I came into the office today, I discovered a donated sax and a note from you about drums."

That day my daughter and I delivered the set to the school. Initially we thought that we were doing a good deed by giving away the drums. We discovered instead that we had stepped into a station. We felt like we were God's stewards, caretakers of *his* drums.

In his great love, God calls us to participate in his ongoing renewal of all things. Moreover, the Lord employs both our weaknesses and our strengths. Our faithful "participation" in stations becomes musiclike praise to God.

Joining God's Symphony

God personally provides our stations. In great and minor ways, God thereby enables us to fulfill divine purposes. Our faithful deeds, in turn, witness to Christ's work in us.

This God-involved call to good works is the pattern throughout the Scriptures, from Adam and Eve through Noah, Esther, Mary, Peter, and Paul. Even the doubting and despondent Job eventually rediscovered his place in God's good works, although he could not figure it out completely. None of us ultimately can—Job was just forthright about his confusion. People don't live long and are "full of trouble," he says. But later he admits that God "can do all things" and no plan of his "can be thwarted."[1]

The Old Testament prophets responded so earnestly to God's call that they frequently got into trouble. They warned unfaithful people to clean up their ways or face harsh judgment. Cut off the heads of all the people—"those who are left I will kill with the sword," Amos tells Israel on God's behalf.[2] Amos was not popular!

The New Testament similarly shows how God equips people for seemingly impractical or even impossible tasks. God grants followers the power of the Holy Spirit so that they can participate faithfully in God's *renewal* of creation.[3] This renewal includes the salvation of souls. But renewal is also our participation with Christ in restoring *all things* to the way that they are supposed to be. Our daily labors might seem insignificant, but they can be important vessels for the work of the Spirit.

God is at work, calling and equipping us for service in particular stations. Paul says that we are "God's workmanship, created in Christ Jesus to do good works, which God prepared in advance for us to do."[4] We are redeemed in Christ in order that we might glorify God with our good deeds, which are already waiting to be accomplished! Even tasks that we perceive as flawed or unimportant can, by God's grace, become part of God's working through us.

It is too easy to assume that God's promises apply only to other people, especially those who seem to walk intimately with the Lord. Paul rejects such spiritual elitism. God saves people for service. Everyone who becomes Jesus's follower is thereby also called to participate in divinely inspired works. Being saved from sin is itself unfathomable, but the Bible shows that all followers receive God-given stations for renewal. Mere mortals are called to be partners under Jesus Christ, just as Abraham became a blessing to future generations.

Here's the stunning imagery of Ephesians 2: God is the perfect conductor of a masterful "Renewed Creation Symphony." Our shared vocation as followers is to "participate" in God's ongoing good works ("workmanship" means literally "art" or "poetry"). Everything we do in each station can be part of this majestic praise of God through the faithful renewal of *all* things.[5]

Renewing "All Things"

Our vocational journey is not made up merely of Bible studies, choir practices, and church services. God invites us to become caretakers of renewal in everything we do, thereby praising God and pointing others to the Lord's good works. In fact, the original meaning of "piety" was faithfulness in everything, not merely in church or devotional practices.

If I am a humble truth teller, for example, I thereby glorify Christ and contribute to God's symphony of restoration. If I forgive others,[6] love mercy, and seek justice for others,[7] I am participating in God's will. When I serve faithfully at my place of employment, I live out my occupational calling. I might even participate in God's symphony of renewal by quitting a job or beginning a new one or by making a wise work decision. My actions will often be far from exceptional, but God will make them perfect after my journey on earth.

Whether we work in education, business, medicine, counseling, or recreation, we can by grace participate in God's renewal of a broken world. Every work station can play a part in our journey toward the New Heaven and New Earth.

Preparing for the *New Heaven* and *New Earth*

Heaven in Scripture is not a faraway place where people play harps and are completely indifferent to earthly reality. Instead the renewal that God has already begun on earth culminates in heaven. As Paul puts it, God is uniting "all things in heaven and on earth together under one head, even Christ."[8] Heaven is the New Jerusalem.[9] God's ongoing renewal on earth prepares the way for his complete renewal of *all* things.

In other words, God will not discard the results of the good deeds that we participate in during this life. Instead he is working through us now as part of his promise to usher in the New Heaven and New Earth—the *New Jerusalem*. "Your labor in the Lord is not in vain," writes Paul.[10]

Isaiah 60 is an amazing description of how God will destroy every form of idolatry while transforming all earthly things into complete praise to the Redeemer. The New Jerusalem in the Scriptures is a real city of justice and peace, without evil and brokenness.

I don't understand exactly *how* followers participate in the renewal of all things. I frequently am humbled by how God uses everyday, seemingly imperfect or insignificant acts of faith to point others to Christ and usher in the New Jerusalem.

Once I was in a major European city with a well-known theologian. After completing a day's work, we were ready to go out for dinner. I suggested a few ethnic cuisines before he interrupted, "You know, I'm having a Big Mac attack."

I was dumbfounded. "Do you mean that you want to go to McDonald's?" I asked. I could not believe it. Here was a theological luminary hankering for a burger in a multicultural city!

"Look," I cautioned, "I'm not sure that God wants us to eat fast food. It isn't healthful."

My theological superior responded, "You sound like a cultural elitist. God is renewing *all* things. The best fast food will be in the New Jerusalem. God will make it perfect."

As we dined on burgers that night, I pondered the meaning of God's renewal of *all* things. Clearly *some* occupational stations are not renewable and should be eliminated: high-stakes gambling, prostitution, terrorism. In addition, there are no perfect professions; they all need renewal. But we ought to be careful about elevating one occupational station above others or assuming that only a handful of superdevout followers will participate in the New Jerusalem.

We are called to participate in God's renewal of many types of labor, leisure, and ministry. A person who enters Christian media needs to take the call to renewal just as seriously as one who works in mainstream radio. In this respect, stations are opportunities for "ministering" to others via the renewal of all things. St. Francis of Assisi encouraged friars to preach with their deeds, not merely or even primarily with their words. St. Augustine wrote that believers should praise God with their whole selves, from head to foot.

In other words, every word and deed can become part of our Christian journey in the world—for good or bad. For example, I find in teaching that everything I do with my students can contribute to or detract from instruction. How I treat them is critically important. Do I listen? Do I genuinely care? Am I their advocate? Do I try to embody the gospel? If not, I am not participating as fully as I should be in the renewal of my teaching, myself, and my students.

This overarching, all-encompassing renewal can seem like an impossible task unless we remember that God is with us, completing our imperfect work. Our stations are God ordained. The Lord promises to make each of us a blessing to others, even in our weaknesses.

Recognizing God in Our Weakness

As part of his renewal of things, God employs our weaknesses as well as our strengths. For instance, God used Paul's bodily imperfection—whatever it was. The apostle even wrote that although his condition was a trial for *others*, the church still received him as an "angel of God."[11] Paul further explained that the "power for us who believe" is a "mighty strength" beyond our

own, human ability.[12] In other words, God calls flawed followers
to stations that seem impossible to participate in well.

Moreover, we will suffer in our weakness because we live in
a broken world filled with conflict and injustice. The writer of
Hebrews describes faithful persons who were tortured, flogged,
jeered, chained, and imprisoned. They were even pierced with
swords and sawed in two. Believers "went about in sheepskins
and goatskins, destitute, persecuted and mistreated. . . . They
wandered in deserts and mountains, and in caves and holes in
the ground."[13]

Today Christians in Africa and other parts of the world face
similar situations. They cry out to God because their circumstances reveal that human beings cannot control their own des-
tinies. In our weaknesses as human beings, we depend utterly
on God.

Those of us in privileged positions of relative wealth and security are not so inclined to admit our limitations. Like King David,
we arrogantly play God, pretending that we can do whatever we
desire. David viewed adultery as a kingly privilege and indirectly
murdered the husband of the woman he seduced.[14] Only after
his repentance did David once again become a great king.

The humble Joseph received increasingly influential stations
over time. He went from being abandoned by his brothers in a
hole to manifesting God's power and grace in his station as the
king's trusted advisor. But it took years of trials in his journey.

Abraham had little going for him when God called. He lacked
a kingly empire. He had gained only moderate wealth with little
social prestige. He was a weak old man, taken advantage of by
his wife. Yet God called Abraham into service far beyond his
human means.

Moses was not a very good public speaker. Perhaps he would
have failed Speech 101. Was his problem a stutter? Stage fright?
Inarticulateness? A tendency to put his foot in his mouth? We
don't know. Scripture merely says he lacked eloquence and was
"slow of speech and tongue."[15]

God appears to Moses as he did to Abraham, Isaac, and Jacob.
The Lord tells Israel's leader that God is going to give the Israelites the Promised Land. But when Moses informs the Israelites, they don't listen because of their "discouragement and
cruel bondage."[16] God responds by giving Moses an even more

difficult station: telling the king of Egypt to free the Israelites from captivity.

Moses then admits his weakness to God: "If the Israelites will not listen to me, why would Pharaoh listen to me, since I speak with faltering lips?"[17] "See," God responds, "I have made you like God to Pharaoh, and your brother Aaron will be your prophet. . . . I will harden Pharaoh's heart, and . . . he will not listen to you. Then I will lay my hand on Egypt and with mighty acts of judgment I will bring out my divisions, my people the Israelites. And the Egyptians will know that I am the LORD when I stretch out my hand against Egypt and bring the Israelites out of it."[18]

I find this story particularly compelling because of my own fear of public speaking. During high school and college, I was petrified in front of groups. I repeatedly made a fool of myself because of my low self-confidence and my debilitating self-consciousness. This is partly why I never seriously considered becoming a teacher. I still surprise myself whenever I seem to be able to communicate with more than a few people.

The biblical Peter is a big talker who seems to lack the capacity to follow through on his rashly made promises. Jesus predicts that Peter will deny his Lord,[19] but Peter still boldly declares his allegiance. Then he does deny knowing his Lord—three times. Peter is the last of the followers to abandon Jesus on the way to the cross—but he still does so.

Peter nonetheless becomes a great follower of Jesus Christ. He heals people and speaks articulately for the faith. Described as an unschooled, ordinary man, Peter nevertheless astonishes crowds.[20]

Mother Teresa, one of the twentieth century's most admired Christians for her selfless work among the poor of Calcutta, lived most of her adult life in spiritual uncertainty and self-doubt. God seemed absent from her at times. She even wondered if the Lord loved her and if her deeds pleased God. Nevertheless, God used her in her darkness to build a worldwide ministry to forgotten and rejected people, including those with HIV/AIDS.

We feeble, self-doubting people are vehicles through whom God communicates his glory. Every human flaw is a "thing" for God to renew.

A pastor told me about a congregation that includes a severely disabled member who can stand only with the aid of a cane. But he is among the most cheerful and infectious worshippers. When the congregation sings "O for a Thousand Tongues to Sing," this man cannot contain his celebration of God's promises. As the choir and congregation praise the Lord in the last stanza, he rises wobbly, waves his cane over his head, and proclaims triumphantly:

> Hear him, ye deaf; His praise, ye dumb,
> Your loosened tongues employ;
> You blind, behold your Savior come;
> And leap, ye lame, for joy.

God calls us in our weaknesses, which become opportunities for God to demonstrate his glory. It's normal to doubt our abilities, but it's also fitting to trust that God can work through our flaws as well as our strengths.

Admitting Our God-Given Strengths

God also employs our strengths in the renewal of all things. He knows us intimately, including our personalities, interests, learned skills, and spiritual abilities. All of these are gifts to use in our various stations.

In spite of what society teaches, our God-given strengths are just as important as formal education. Some college students wrongly decide on academic majors merely according to what they "want to be," regardless of their strengths. A culture of *individual choice* dominates middle- and upper-middle-class society.

The freedom to choose occupational stations is far superior to systems limited by social class or academic achievements. Nevertheless, we need to embrace this freedom wisely, recognizing that personal desires and academic degrees best supplement our deeper gifts.

Human *gifts* can include *God-given capacities, personal traits,* and *learned skills*. All of our general talents and spiritual gifts ultimately are presents *from* God and *for* serving in God's world. We are called to identify and develop our God-given gifts so that we can care more fully for God's world.

Identifying Our Root Gifts

God gives us gifts to enjoy and use. Sometimes the job market might make it difficult to find ways of exercising them in our vocational stations, but if we identify our *root gifts*—those applicable across many different stations—we are much more likely to discover satisfying work. Root gifts include such things as empathizing, analyzing, organizing, diagnosing, designing, encouraging, and persuading. But how do we identify our own root gifts?

First, we can identify root gifts by trying out apparent strengths. A potentially gifted listener, for example, might listen to the stories of friends and family—asking follow-up questions, re-telling their stories back to them, or even editing a short video or audio recording of someone telling her or his story. A person with this potential gift might even try a part-time job or volunteer experience that would require significant listening, such as telephone-based customer support, where visual cues are completely absent.

Second, we can identify root gifts by considering our interests. Often what people truly like to do—not just what they think they like to do—will reveal gifts. We frequently learn to enjoy particular activities, whether hobbies or work, because we are naturally good at them.

A student was a gifted writer with a heart for justice. Since she also enjoyed writing, I was not surprised that after graduation she entered communication. As opportunities opened up and she matured, however, she felt called to address an important issue from her own life—abuse. Eventually she used her gift of writing to compose materials about abuse and even to launch a ministry to help victims. Clearly her interest in communication was widely transferable. So was her heart for justice.

Third, we can identify root gifts by reviewing past work and volunteer experiences. I ask people who are exploring new stations to compose a special résumé that reflects their life experiences, not just their employment. Hobbies, volunteer activities, family experiences, and extracurricular interests can be very self-instructive.

One of my mentees included a résumé line about taking care of siblings. Probing a bit, I discovered that she was the primary

caretaker for two younger sisters during her mother's long bout
with cancer. We discovered that her success at this task over
several years reflected root gifts such as patience, perseverance,
and organization.

*Fourth, we can identify root gifts by conferring with those we
know and trust.* What do others see as our strengths? What have
they noticed about us? What do they most admire in us? Friends
and co-workers who will answer honestly in love are a special
blessing. But we need to give them opportunities to do so—to
invite them to join our journey toward greater self-awareness
and candid self-assessment.

*Fifth, we can gain a more complete understanding of our in-
terests and traits by taking standardized "tests."* Psychological,
personality, and occupational instruments can help. Most schools
and job agencies offer them.

Conclusion

God uses followers' strengths and weaknesses to participate
in their deeds. Moses's faith was not enough to make him a self-
confident speaker, so God gave him Aaron as a spokesperson.
King David was courageous, but he ultimately needed more
humility; God used David's confession to call him back to faithfulness. Mary's humble faith, remarkable patience, and deep
courage defined her character as the chosen mother of Jesus
Christ. Peter's sincerity was offset by his impulsiveness, but by
grace he became a great leader.

The Scriptures are filled with stories of dysfunctional families,
corrupted leaders, and wayward followers. God calls followers
when they are in the muck of real life, where families feud and
religious people often fail. God's wisdom is complete as he directs
ordinary people to participate in extraordinary work, even if the
tasks seem useless, unrealistic, or mundane. This is the nature
of vocational journeys.

Our weakness and giftedness become, through faith, part of
God's grand symphony of renewal that blesses current and future
generations. Scripture puts it this way: "By faith Abraham, when
called to go to a place he would later receive as his inheritance,
obeyed and went, even though he did not know where he was

going."[21] Abraham could not see the future clearly, but he trusted that the God who called him would also lead him. Abraham thereby became one of God's followers. "And so from this one man, and he as good as dead, came descendants as numerous as the stars in the sky and as countless as the sand on the sea-shore."[22] This result must have been music to God's ears as well as a laughable surprise to Abraham.

A seemingly minor calling, such as offering to donate a drum set to a school, requires little skill. In God's plan, however, even what appears to be a relatively minor station can be a vehicle for renewing others' lives through the work of the Spirit.

3

Succeeding Wholeheartedly

The handwritten note read as follows:

Carol,

I am so sorry for this. I feel I just cannot go on. I have always tried to do the right thing but where there was once great pride now its [sic] gone. I love you and the children so much. I just cannot be any good to you or myself. The pain is overwhelming. Please try to forgive me.

A successful executive wrote this to his wife before committing suicide. He had already resigned from his company, which was under investigation for fraud.

Tragic news stories show that human achievements can fade quickly. Even after we achieve fame or fortune, we might be very restless, unhappy, and unfulfilled.

Earthly success can be the fruit of selfish or faithful efforts—or both. Public achievement often obscures private failures, whereas public failure can cloud personal faithfulness. Although God uses our strengths and weaknesses, the only lasting measure of success is faithfulness. Everything done in faith has enduring

value. A follower of Jesus Christ obeys the call to give her or his
heart to God in faith.

Opening Our Hearts

Author and priest Henri M. Nouwen describes how he left a
prestigious academic station at Harvard University to serve a
Canadian community that cares for emotionally and physically
disabled persons. For him, the academic status, high profile, and
competitive spirit of his university position made it increasingly
difficult to open his heart to God and others. "Our society is not
a community radiant with the love of Christ," he writes, "but a
dangerous network of domination and manipulation in which
we can easily get entangled and lose our soul."

Although Nouwen probably overstates his case, he rightly
focuses on the role of the heart in vocational living. The most
important decisions in life are matters of the heart. Our hearts
reflect our innermost attitudes and deepest convictions, such
as how we feel about failure, guilt, love, and redemption.[1] The
concept of opening my heart to Jesus Christ is a way of saying
that I want my whole being to conform to the Lord's will so that
my life's journey is toward a deeper relationship with God.[2]

The Psalms show us that our hearts direct our thoughts and
actions. These songs describe people whose hearts are upright,
sorrowful, or filled with destruction. The Psalms proclaim that
we should live with the truth in our hearts; that God probes
our hearts; that the Lord wants us to have clean and meditative
hearts; that our hearts should leap for joy as we praise God;
that we should live with God's law in our hearts; and that we
are called to pursue God with our whole heart.[3]

In order to hear and live out God's callings, we must regularly
renew our hearts for service. This is not a matter of "feelings"
as much as trust and commitment. "Wholehearted" renewal
means that we admit our failures, accept Jesus's ravishing love
for us, bathe our hearts thankfully in God's grace, and commit
ourselves to lifelong service under the lordship of Christ. In
short, by grace we become living sacrifices.[4] Author Madeleine
L'Engle, for instance, says that a faithful writer must "die to
self" or else nothing good will be born from the resulting essay

or book. If we die to self, she says, "no matter how frightened we may be, we will be found and born anew into life, and life more abundant." By offering our hearts to God, promptly and sincerely, we heed God's call to become living sacrifices in all of our caretaking.

Opening our hearts is the first step toward working out our faith with "fear and trembling."[5] "Walking the talk" is a cliché, but the need is genuine. Unless we open our hearts to God, we will merely pursue our own ambitions. A faithful follower offers her or his heart to God. Then a follower's mind and body can follow the heart on vocational journeys.

Putting Our Hearts into Our Stations

My first paid job was cleaning and restocking shelves in a family drugstore. After one week, I had mastered the work and grown bored. Then two things began to improve my view of the tedious job: customers started asking *me* where to find products, and I noticed shoppers purchasing items that *I* had restocked. The paycheck was useful, whereas serving others was rewarding.

Because we are creatures of the heart, we seek work and volunteer stations that serve others. Our labor need not be impressive, but it is most gratifying when it contributes to others' well-being. Nearly all work has this potential.

My wife and I decided to design a beautiful backyard in a sunken area that was filled with mud and stones and could not support plants. So we ordered some new soil and hired a bulldozer operator to fill up the mud pit and contour the area. He quickly transformed our mucky mess into an attractive flower spot. Afterwards I told him that he is an artist and the earth is his medium. Clearly his heart was in his work. We now love the renewed yard. And we hope that he found pleasure both in his labor and in our gratitude.

Jesus Christ addresses the role of heart in stations when a lawyer asks him a compelling question: "What must I do to inherit eternal life?" Jesus responds that one must love God, neighbor, and self with all of her or his heart.[6] Wholehearted work, for instance, requires loving God and others, not just earning a wage or salary. This language of the heart does not mean that we all should seek nonprofit service jobs, such as teaching, ministry, and counseling. A plumber, bus driver, housekeeper, physical therapist, drummer, and retail clerk can love wholeheartedly too. So can an entrepreneur, a politician, and a chemist. All stations provide opportunities for wholehearted service.

Recently I rode on a city bus in San Diego. The middle-aged, African-American driver was a remarkable servant. She greeted us with a sincere smile, offered advice about local places to visit, and asked the busload of people what they thought about city and world affairs. She cracked witty jokes and told us all how thankful she was for her job of twenty-three years. "There's nothing I would rather do," she declared. "I love my passengers." She mentioned that she had turned down office work in order to continue serving her riders.

Then an elderly Asian man walked from the back to the front of the bus to place trash in a small bucket. The driver complimented him for keeping the bus clean, smiled, and leaned into the aisle. He then leaned toward her while facing the back of the bus, and she kissed him lightly on the cheek. Passengers broke out in applause. During this short trip, the driver's heart transformed the vehicle into a station for civility, service, and joy.

Avoiding Riches and Prestige

Two major corrupting desires can diminish our capacity to participate wholeheartedly in our stations. One is the drive for stations with *prestige*. The other is an unquenchable thirst for earthly *riches*. When either desire settles in our hearts, it sours our life and labor. Overcoming these two temptations requires learning how to pursue our callings *in* the world without becoming people *of* the world.[7]

First, society establishes a deceptive hierarchy of stations that overemphasizes prestige. Within the church, for instance, Christians tend to revere megachurch leaders more than those who work tirelessly in smaller congregations. We look up to celebrity authors and Christian media stars and musical performers. The early church had this problem too, as some church leaders were more interested in creating their own followings than in teaching others to follow Christ.[8]

We all tend to judge particular occupational stations based on widely held stereotypes. Forty years ago, entering the ministry or teaching was a revered goal. Now such endeavors are not nearly so popular or prestigious. Many people see medicine as a worthy station, while law is mocked. Construction laborers and letter carriers don't fare as well as airline pilots and business executives.

We judge individuals according to nonoccupational stations too. If people "stay home with the kids," we might give them a polite nod of affirmation. But we probably wonder why they have not done more with their lives. Gender stereotypes also cloud our thinking about the value of particular stations in society. A mother who cares for children at home is likely to be more respected than a father who does

Racial stereotypes, social class, marital status, and ethnic biases shape perceptions of prestige as well. The unemployed frequently are pitied and quietly criticized for alleged lack of self-discipline even when they are victims of economic decline or poor governmental policies. Single parents, often struggling to make ends meet, are viewed as second-class members of many congregations. Young Mary's station as the pregnant mother of Jesus lacked social prestige. Wealthy executives are dismissed as selfish.

Even this book reflects particular social assumptions about work and other stations. I have a prestigious professorial position that provides time to read, contemplate, and write about vocation, whereas many people are struggling to make a decent living. People call me "Dr. Schultze" and honor me more than I am worthy of receiving. I have to remind myself frequently that I have benefited from God's grace and social privilege and that earthly prestige alone does not merit any honor in God's kingdom.

Contrary to our stereotypes, there are no perfect occupations worthy of uncritical acceptance. Every social institution and all occupations need renewal. In addition, even a person who attains an impressive position in a highly respected, service-oriented field can succumb to heartlessness. Paul was converted *from* a respected "religious" life *to* a station of faithful ministry. He lost prestige and gained a lot of hardship.

A friend who earned a dental degree decided to work in the inner city for a while. When he visited urban practices, however, he discovered that some dentists were defrauding the government on medical insurance and failing to practice adequate hygiene with disadvantaged patients. He realized that even the most respected stations can give heartless persons and organizations a means to exploit others.

Striving selfishly for prestige is the opposite of caretaking. Paul tells us to think of other people as better than ourselves.[9] He reminds us that Jesus Christ "made himself nothing" and became "a servant."[10] Seeking others' approval can trap us into caring more about ourselves than others.[11]

Besides, prestige does not guarantee happiness. When I was a college student, a young humanities professor befriended me. We met in his office and at his home, discussing life beyond the classroom. I discovered that he had given up a law career to teach history. I admired him.

One night he died after taking recreational drugs. Reflecting on his life, I recalled him telling me that the nicest person in his campus building was the janitor. "He's the only honest guy in this place. Nearly everyone else is phony." Then the professor pulled open a file drawer and lifted out a quart of beer. "Some nights the two of us share a glass," he said.

Here was a professor who, in my naïve judgment, had achieved the good life. He had earned a doctoral degree and become a faculty member at a prestigious research university. Yet down deep he was a lonely, disheartened person. The self-importance of academe was painfully apparent to him. Prestige didn't meet his need for a meaningful work station.

Certainly we should look up to, admire, and even follow those whose lives are worthy. After all, we are created to be followers, leaders, and mentors, to nurture and guide one another. But who and why we follow are crucially important. Honor, not prestige, should direct our attention.

Second, we can corrupt our stations by falling prey to an unquenchable thirst for earthly riches. Work, for example, can be a legitimate means of earning a living, enjoying the fruits of one's labor, and creating wealth for serving others. When our hearts desire wealth above everything else, however, we love riches more than God, neighbor, and self. We mistakenly live by the motto that the person who dies with the most toys wins. The fact is that all riches are fleeting and offer no long-term satisfaction or deep inner peace. Only a fool lives primarily for riches.

Scripture says that the love of riches is the root of evil.[12] This distorted love denies God's ultimate ownership of our talents and possessions. If our heart's first love is something in the creation rather than the Creator, we become idolaters, with little space left in our hearts for God or neighbor. Our careless journey becomes a dead-end street. In effect, we merely call ourselves into selfishness.

I know a man who inherited a profitable business from his generous parents. He lives well, but restlessly, unable to find comfort in his wealth. He even asks friends for their meal receipts after sharing a personal lunch, so that he can illegally submit their expenses for his own business reimbursement. He simply cannot put enough money into his pockets, even though he really doesn't need more. Sadly, he treasures the accumulation of riches that he has not even earned. Nothing satisfies his thirst for more. He lives as if he has been called to greed.

"For where your treasure is, there your heart will be also," says Jesus.[13] Prestige and riches are false treasures. The traitor Judas evidently had both, whereas the faithful Peter had neither one. Judas eventually hanged himself, whereas Peter became a great caretaker of the church. So Jesus calls us to consider all that we have and to follow him.[14] In other words, we should seek first the kingdom of God. Then we will recognize all resulting wealth and honor as gifts and responsibilities rather than as ends in themselves.

Monitoring Our Hearts

All of us struggle with desires for prestige and riches. No matter how much we have, we desire more. If we lose our hearts to them during our journey, however, we are bound to feel restless and unsatisfied. We should monitor our hearts by considering three vocational danger signs.

First, corrupted desires slowly worsen over time. Selfishness grows and blossoms later in life, gradually distorting how persons understand the purposes of their stations. Love of neighbor eventually gives way to love of self. Sometimes we even use God's name to justify the change: "The Lord has blessed me"; "If poor people trusted God, they could be successful too." Is our vocational journey moving in a selfless or selfish direction?

Second, an immoderate desire for riches or prestige robs our hearts of gratitude. Earning wealth and prestige can make us humble and fill us with joy if we maintain hearts of gratitude to God rather than boasting about our own abilities. On the other hand, success can overwhelm our hearts, turning us into impatient, arrogant persons. Often there is a fine line between a legitimate sense of achievement and thankless pride. Do we know where that line is in our own stations?

Third, prestige and riches don't provide spiritual resources for dealing with inevitable failure. All of us will make mistakes, even prominent errors of judgment that we will regret our whole lives. Most frustrating of all, failure sometimes occurs as a result of events that we cannot control.

Many respected leaders admit that their accomplishments resulted from opportunities as well as from their own efforts. Moreover, they concede that they succeeded in spite of the mistakes they made along the way. Finally, they suggest that the times of gross error were the most difficult periods in their lives. How they handled failure during their journeys, they say, formed their characters just as much as how they dealt with success.

One of the great mysteries of Christian vocation is that followers of Jesus do suffer. Although suffering can teach us to depend more on God and less on ourselves, it is rarely a joy. Paradoxically, true freedom in Christ includes being at liberty to fail. "Blessed are the poor in spirit," says Jesus, "for theirs is the kingdom of heaven."[15] Paul even says we are heirs in suffering with Christ.[16]

There is nothing wrong with desiring good academic or work evaluations, seeking appropriate salary raises, earning job promotions, appreciating friends who admire us, and seeking worthy change. Yet disappointment, more than achievement, prompts us to open our hearts to God so that we can grow in faith as well as participate in truly good works. When we respond to our failures faithfully, we remind ourselves that God loves us even in our brokenness. We are God's *beloved*. He suffers with us as well as for us.

Paul wrote from jail that believers should be content in all circumstances.[17] For Paul, heartfelt contentment was a sign of trust in God, not a measure of earthly success. Paul's letter addressed a church located along an important trade route, near fertile land and gold mines. The congregation that heard his letter read in worship likely represented the range of people found in major cities—wealthy, poor, admired, and forsaken. They probably recognized just how countercultural Paul's message was for their day—just as it should be heard in our time.

Are we ready and willing to suffer for Christ? Or do we increasingly seek comfort and ease instead? We are not called to pursue suffering for the sake of suffering, but instead to accept the kind of suffering that inevitably accompanies vocational living. During such suffering, God and friends ease our burden by suffering with us.

Conclusion

We can become so heartlessly dedicated to earthly success that we no longer see our stations as gifts from God and opportunities to sacrifice for others. We can even end up laboring merely for personal gain, hopping from job to job or relationship to relationship without deeper satisfaction, determined to get ahead at whatever cost to our souls.[18] As a result, we might fall into *consumerism* (earning money solely to spend it selfishly) or *narcissism* (doing whatever makes us feel good and makes us temporarily happy). Selfish desires are unfulfilling substitutes for selfless faithfulness.

We need to remind ourselves regularly why and for whom we ultimately live. Real success has nothing directly to do with prestige or riches. Instead success is the process of seeking first the kingdom of God.[19] A true follower has heard, accepted, and begun acting upon the call to care wholeheartedly for God's world in every station.

4

Caring Responsibly

William Rodriguez was a kickboxing champion as well as a black belt in karate. He knew how to fight and win. Even so, when gang members killed his son, Rodriguez refused to respond violently. He didn't even seek revenge. Instead he sought a just and lasting reconciliation.

After discovering that one of his son's convicted killers was wrongly sentenced, Rodriguez asked the judge for mercy on the young man. "I just believed it was the right thing to do. That's my faith," he recalled.

Rodriguez's desire for justice led him to a new station. As a result of his involvement in his son's murder trial, he began orchestrating peace treaties among warring gangs. The kickboxer spoke to feuding groups about living for the future rather than in bondage to the past. Seeing that Rodriguez was living that message, many gang members listened. Soon Rodriguez was hosting reconciliatory meetings. To his own surprise, he became a channel of peaceful renewal.

Rodriguez's station of peacemaking illustrates human beings' overarching vocation as followers of Jesus Christ. Just as God cares for his entire universe, we are called to be caretakers of God's world. God calls us to love Jesus Christ by caring *for* and *about* our neighbor. When we live faithfully as caretakers under God's authority, our many stations become opportunities for us to participate in Jesus Christ's renewal of all things.

Caring in All Stations

An expert in Jewish law asks Jesus Christ how to inherit eternal life. Jesus answers with the parable of the good Samaritan, the story of an Israelite who is robbed, stripped, beaten, and left for dead along the side of a road. Two religious people pass by the man rather than offering help.

Then a Samaritan—a member of a people despised for provoking the Israelites—assists the needy traveler. The Samaritan dresses the Jew's body and wounds, takes him to an inn, and gives the keeper money to continue caring for the man. After Jesus tells this parable, he instructs the lawyer to imitate the Samaritan.[1]

This revolutionary story suggests that our vocation as Jesus's followers challenges practically everything we tend to pursue: self-gain, clannishness, self-righteousness, and personal safety. The Samaritan risked his life, sacrificed his own time and money, and opened his heart to a person from a hated culture. He responsibly lived out the overall vocation of caretaking.

Like us, the Samaritan was called to be a caretaker in God's world. Although he was not a medical or religious expert, and therefore not the most qualified to address the man's body and spirit, the Samaritan realized that the man's problem was also his problem. The Samaritan's relationship to God is unclear, but he cared more than the religious leaders who failed to help.

Followers of Jesus Christ are called to be responsible caretakers in all stations. Our overall vocation is to care for God's world. As theologian Cornelius Plantinga Jr. puts it, we are called to be *prime citizens* who passionately care for the kingdom of God.

The biblical concept of "care" is so diluted in society today that we need to reclaim its roots. Already in Genesis 2, we read that God put Adam in the Garden of Eden to "take care of it." Later, human beings are called to care for God's law and thereby love the Lord. Just as God cares for us, we are to care for God's sheep.[2] Each one of us is created to glorify God by caring for "every square inch" of God's world.

In this biblical framework, God equips us to be vessels of his care. The Creator God gives us the bodies to act in the world, Jesus Christ offers us and shows us renewed minds, and the Holy Spirit grants us caring hearts. When we look across a congregation during worship, we might even imagine a sanctuary full of actor-caretakers, machinist-caretakers, teacher-caretakers, businessperson-caretakers, scientist-caretakers, and many others.

By the grace of the Triune God, wholehearted caring transforms our compensated or volunteer stations into royal service under the King. God redeems us and invites us to a partnership in this divine purpose. "All things" are ours for caring service.[3] Each station offers an opportunity to participate "carefully" in the renewal of his broken world.[4]

I once took an old car to an auto-glass company because the driver's-side window crank was broken. The proprietor informed me that he didn't normally fix window mechanisms, but he invited me to drive my car into his garage anyway, since no customers were waiting for service. He and his partner labored on my vehicle for forty-five minutes, eventually repairing the window crank. When they finished the job, I discovered that they had no intention of charging me for the service. "You'll come back when you need some glass," the manager said as he waved good-bye to me. Using his heart, mind, and body, he took care of my problem.

Living in a needy world, we will discover plenty of stations for caring. God sees to it. The issue is whether or not we will accept the call to care responsibly under God's authority.

Being Responsible Owners under God

Martin Luther King Jr. told the story of a wise preacher who delivered the graduation speech at a college. After his address, the preacher conversed with a brilliant graduate named Robert.

"What are your plans for the future, Robert?"

"I plan to go immediately to law school."

"What then, Robert?"

"Well . . . I plan to get married and start a family."

"What then, Robert?"

"I must frankly say that I plan to make lots of money from my law practice, and thereby I hope to retire rather early and spend a great deal of time traveling to various parts of the world."

"What then, Robert?"

"Well . . . these are most of my plans."

Finally, the preacher replied, "Young man, your plans are far too small. They can extend only seventy-five or a hundred years at the most. You must make your plans big enough to include God and large enough to include eternity."

Like Robert, we tend to concoct short-term, egocentric plans. We think in small, secular terms, wrongly assuming that the world is merely ours and that we humans can determine the future apart from God. As a result, we fail to care for the world as God's special creation.

True caretakers accept responsibility for others' needs under God's authority. The Samaritan acknowledged personal responsibility for the problem that he discovered on his journey, even though he didn't create the problem. By contrast, the robbers stole clothes and money and nearly took a life. They acted as if the man and his possessions belonged to them rather than ultimately to God. From a biblical perspective, the Samaritan was moved by mercy and therefore sought justice for the man. Although he could not immediately do anything about the robbers, he could help to restore the man's life. Based on his actions, not just his feelings of sympathy, the Samaritan could give an account for his stewardship.[5]

Accepting responsibility under God is like being a steward who acts on behalf of the owner of an estate. For instance, a democratic leader should act justly for the good of the people rather than for special interests. A CEO is called to represent fairly the interests of stockholders, customers, employees, and the broader society—even though addressing these groups' sometimes conflicting interests will be difficult. Teachers are obliged to care for students as heirs of the future, not just as sources of tuition revenue. Ministers should tend to their flocks as representatives of the Great Shepherd. In each station, caring is a greater good than self-interest, and the highest form of such caring is serving others as God has supplied us with stations.

The church historically formalized this kind of caretaking in the station of the *curate* or *curator*. Just as an art museum relies on a curator to be responsible for the collecting and displaying of artifacts, a church curator accepts responsibility for the "care of the souls" of members. He might teach, preach, and visit the sick. But the curator's primary role is to equip others to do likewise by caring for the building, grounds, and finances so that the ministry of the church can occur. Every follower of Jesus Christ is called to be a curator within some stations and always under the ultimate authority of God.

If we reject this higher calling, we become carelessly selfish. For example, we might drive recklessly, speeding, skipping stop signs, and throwing trash out of car windows. Instead we should drive carefully, leaving notes of apology and responsibility when we ding someone else's vehicle. We should offer rides to friends when they are emotionally distraught, are overly tired, or have been drinking. By God's grace, we can accept our own vehicle and driver's license as gifts for caretaking.

All worthy things, ideas, and skills that we possess are gifts intended to be used and enjoyed in tune with this divine purpose of caretaking. Although we will never use them flawlessly since we are imperfect creatures, we should aim to employ them responsibly. The Protestant Reformer John Calvin (1509–1564) says that we are called to be "stewards of everything God has conferred on us by which we are able to help our neighbor." He adds that "right stewardship" is "tested by the rule of love."

Responsible ownership under God is our task in every area of life. Who are we? We are caretakers, responsible for using our gifts to praise God by serving others. Why were we created? To praise God in personal and corporate worship as well as to praise him by caring for his world. How do we care for God's world? We care by accepting the Lord's ultimate ownership of all things, serving our neighbors responsibly, sharing God's Word, and spreading his kingdom by caretaking within every station.

Who is our role model? First and foremost, we are called to imitate Jesus Christ, whose own journey to the cross demonstrates that he cares selflessly for us. Jesus is *the* model of excellence and compassion—two aspects of Christian caring.

Caring with *Excellence* and *Compassion*

Christians have long established institutions of care for people of all faiths. Most hospitals were started by churches and denominations. So were nearly all private colleges and universities and many domestic and international relief agencies, neighborhood associations, food banks, employment agencies, and drug rehabilitation clinics. In some parts of North America, Christian businesspersons formed associations to conduct retailing, manufacturing, and wholesaling as responsible caretakers of God's resources.

The biblical concept of *care* is not confined to the helping professions, such as ministry, nonprofit, or voluntary work. Caring demonstrates human beings' unique capacity to love God, creation, others, and ourselves. *Excellence* (skillfully caring *for*) and *compassion* (empathically caring *about*) are two major aspects of responsible caring.

First, we are called to care for others excellently. This is the technical aspect of caretaking. The more skilled we are, the better we can serve others.

History documents Christians' attention to skilled excellence in many endeavors, including academic scholarship, literature, and scientific investigation. Christian groups established universities, such as Harvard, Yale, and Princeton. C. S. Lewis, known for popular writings like *Mere Christianity* and *The Screwtape Letters*, was also a respected scholar of literature. Aleksandr Solzhenitsyn's outstanding literary vision reflects his Christian worldview. Galileo (1564–1642) was a devout Christian and skilled physicist who challenged the popular assumption that the earth was the center of the universe.

This call to excellence should guarantee that Christian art and entertainment are particularly well crafted, but frequently it does not. Often Christians make inferior imitations of broader culture rather than their own, excellent products. Christian music, movies, television programs, and novels tend to be second-rate versions of nonreligious products.

Although our efforts should not be arrogantly elitist, they should reflect skilled caretaking. Seeking Christian excellence partly means striving for the finest work, the best service, the most beautiful production—the "most excellent way," to borrow Paul's phrase.[6]

Such excellence is not perfection. Nor is it a reason for boasting. Excellence is *excelling*—doing our very best with the education and training available to us. This is why it is so critically important for us to identify and develop our gifts, always with a realistic view of our internal and external limits, from available resources to our level of authority.

I visited a Christian friend who was in the hospital recovering from knee surgery. He spoke glowingly of his surgeon as an expert in knee replacement. "I'd rather have a skilled non-Christian than an inferior believer for a surgeon," he remarked. I agreed. But I also wondered about all of the other people involved in good medical practice, from radiologists to nurses, from billing clerks to hospital administrators. The range of skills necessary to make my friend's surgery a success is staggering. A hospital, like a society or church, best functions when everyone pursues excellence in his or her occupational station. Whenever that occurs, a kind of miracle takes place.

The good Samaritan was a first-rate caretaker. He took his time to attend to the man's wounds. He delivered the injured traveler safely to the inn and paid the keeper to guarantee that the wounded stranger would have continued rest and help. He promised to reimburse the proprietor for any additional expenses. The good Samaritan served admirably as a nurse, taxi driver, bodyguard, brother, and insurer.

Paul authored one of the most amazing statements about the mind and heart of an excellent caretaker: "Whatever is true, whatever is noble, whatever is right, whatever is pure, whatever is lovely, whatever is admirable—if anything is excellent or praiseworthy—think about such things."[7]

Second, we are called to care compassionately. We glorify God by being kindhearted, empathic servants in all stations. Paul urges followers to clothe themselves with compassion.[8] Compassion means "suffering with." Probably the greatest list of traits of compassion is the fruits of the Spirit: love, joy, peace, patience, kindness, goodness, faithfulness, gentleness, and self-control.[9] These are critical for caring about others.

God gives us capacities for empathy and sympathy. Such gifts enable us to care about others even as they care about us. We are not meant to journey as lone or indifferent followers of Jesus but rather to offer and accept compassion. Simone Weil, author of astonishing essays on God's love, said that the "capacity to give one's attention to a sufferer is a very rare and difficult thing; it is almost a miracle; it *is* a miracle."

In my station as a college professor, for instance, I am called to care about students. When I listen to them, I discover how they feel about life, not just about school. I learn that many are anxious about God's will. They sense that personal success is not a satisfactory purpose in life, but they usually are uncertain about how to proceed. Many suffer anxiety about their futures. In order to care about them, I have to tune my heart to their hopes and fears. Even though I am not a psychologist—and I do need to be aware of my limitations—I am called to teach *persons*, not merely *courses*, *lessons*, or *classes*.

Caring about others is especially difficult in professions in which people are stressed out, mistakes can have major consequences, and overspecialization can reduce caring to technical skill. A compassionate as well as skilled family doctor says that many patients today seek physicians who care "for *them*, not just their organs."

I once conducted focus groups for an advertising agency that was spending plenty on radio commercials for a bank. The agency asked me to determine how consumers were reacting to the ads. I recruited participants and discovered that the commercials offended nearly all listeners. Concerned about the impact of the ads on the bank's image and bottom line, I quickly wrote up my report and presented it to the agency.

Months later, I still heard the ads on the radio, so I called the agency to find out what had transpired since it received my report. I was stunned to discover that the agency never shared my conclusions with its client. The agency did not want to risk losing the bank's business by admitting its mistake.

I had tried to care about the agency, the client, and the public—but seemingly to no avail. In my view, the bank had a great product, but the agency did not care enough about its client to produce audience-sensitive ads. Moreover, the agency failed to accept its responsibility to be truthful to the bank.

Should I have done more—such as contacting the client directly? I don't know. Maybe I lacked courage. Or maybe such contact was not my responsibility. I was paid well for my work. Why should I have cared that the client might have suffered lower revenues?

So much of life seems relatively trivial with little need for compassion. But maybe this is precisely our problem in more affluent parts of the world. We become self-absorbed in our own, fairly minor "suffering" while much of the world even in our own backyards truly suffers from joblessness, racism, poor education, inadequate housing, no medical or other insurance, persecution, political and ethical violence, HIV/AIDS, hunger, and so much more.

How can we followers of Jesus Christ not heed the call to empathetic compassion as well as skilled excellence? Surely we can quibble about when and how to care, but if we are not willing to suffer with those who suffer, we are lukewarm caretakers. Sometimes we need to hear Christ asking us sobering questions: whom are you willing to suffer with? To die for?

Caring for Self

We are not called to care so selflessly that we hurt ourselves emotionally, spiritually, or physically. Self-sacrificial care is not the same as careless self-destruction. We need only to offer the most excellent care, using the gifts that God has granted us. The rest is up to God and other caretakers.

Yet God does promise to care for us as we care for others. Paul suggests that we should expect the peace of God when we seek excellence.[10] This is an amazing personal benefit to caring, although it ought not be our motivation. We might achieve great riches and impressive prestige, but the one thing that we can count on in the long run is God's peace in the midst of our brokenness. That peace is a taste of heaven on earth.

Tasting Heaven on Earth

I wonder what the traveler felt when he awoke at the inn after the good Samaritan had cared for him. He was probably surprised. Then perhaps he was worried about how he would pay for his care—until he heard from the innkeeper that all expenses were covered. He must have been deeply gratified. Each caring act becomes a sign that points others to the kingdom of God.

Eventually the man must have been surprised by joy. Even in his great misfortune, he probably began to have a bit of hope for peace between the mutually antagonistic Israelites and Samaritans. The traveler was nearly killed, but thanks to the Samaritan, he tasted a bit of heavenly renewal on earth.

So why do we not post more heavenward signs? For one thing, we recall times when others took advantage of our caring spirit and actions. For another, care seems very impractical. We are so results-driven that caring strikes us as ineffective, especially in competitive marketplaces. Finally, we get overly busy and distracted by day-to-day tasks. Figuring out how to act responsibly in some stations requires adequate time, discernment, and advice from others.

Works of care please God, however, and most of the time they matter to those whom we serve. We all can recall times when we received help from a kind friend, parent, neighbor, or passerby. But the parable of the good Samaritan doesn't address the beaten man's response, probably because it doesn't matter. Caring skillfully for and compassionately about others is simply the right way for Jesus's followers to live. It is faith in God's power to work through our responsible action.

Caring also radiates hope. Whenever we care, we become carriers of the hope that is in Jesus Christ. In a sobering passage on responsibility, Jesus ties faithfulness to caring. He says that individuals who truly care about small things are likely to care about greater things. And those who don't care about little things are likely to squander major ones.[11] Human beings tend either to waste or to invest their God-given blessings. The ability to care is a special gift from God that we ought not to squander because of our own fear, indifference, or laziness.

A friend and exceptional student at a Christian college received a grade of C on what was probably an A paper. The teacher wrote this comment under the grade: "To whom much is given, much shall be required."[12]

Although my friend expressed her dislike of being evaluated according to a higher standard, I admitted to her that I occasionally grade this way. My intent, however poorly executed,

is simply to encourage and reward students in tune with their
giftedness, so that they learn to bring as much excellence as
possible to earth. But I admitted that I can easily misapply this
standard. Some situations call for balancing excellence and
compassion. It is not easy.

Caretaking is being compassionate and excellent in our stations, not trying to be perfectionists. On earth we can taste
heaven, but we are not able to enjoy Jesus's full banquet of delight
no matter how hard we try.

Conclusion

In his stirring autobiography about Japanese prison camps
during World War II, Allied soldier Ernest Gordon describes a
caring friendship that developed between a cobbler and an engineer. The engineer had an inventive mind while the cobbler was
skilled with his hands. Together they walked around the prison
yard discussing a secret project.

Then one day the two informed other prisoners that they had
designed and manufactured an artificial leg. The prosthesis was
"a workmanlike article," says Gordon. The foot was a block of
wood secured to a bamboo leg with strips of metal from old cans,
tied together with leather. The leg supported a basket of leather
and canvas designed to hold the person's stump. An ingenious
tin joint served as the knee.

Prisoners were amazed and delighted. Here was an invention
that would serve many prisoners who had lost legs in battle or
in forced labor. "With mobility and work to fill the idle hours
came new hope," writes Gordon. Passing the production area
one evening, Gordon heard a strange sound and turned to see "a
cocky little man strutting proudly along on two artificial legs."

"That's quite a performance you're giving," said Gordon
admiringly.

"You haven't seen nothing yet," replied the prisoner outfit-
ted with manufactured limbs. "Keep your eye on me. When
I get these pistons working properly, I'll be the fastest man in
camp."

Caring for and about God's world is our overarching calling
as followers of Jesus Christ. Each act of care reflects the hope

of Jesus Christ to those who need it. Such caring is a heavenly responsibility, as the good Samaritan demonstrated, as Rodriguez discovered while orchestrating peace among rival gangs in Los Angeles, and as Gordon found while living in seemingly hopeless confinement. As we respond gratefully to God's grace in our own lives, we are motivated to care for and about others in Jesus's name.

5

Celebrating Leisure

A few years ago, my wife and I decided to take a break from three decades of work in order to refocus our lives. Our children were both in college, and I was eligible for an academic sabbatical. We moved to Florida for nine months of personal study and spiritual renewal.

Because we had few friends in the area, we faced only a few daily tasks, such as preparing meals, getting the mail, and reading the newspaper. Except for my wife's weekly volunteer day and our Sunday worship, we had no fixed schedule.

Our time of rest went better than planned. In addition to making excellent progress on our projects, we renewed our relationships with each other, God, and nature. We prayed much together. We observed the wildlife on a small lake behind our condo, even befriending a great blue heron. After hunting for food each morning, he would settle outside our porch for an afternoon nap, resting on one leg. He reminded us that life is peace as well as plans.

Leisure-related stations are critically important for the renewal of all of our caretaking in other stations. Because Jesus has done what we could never do for ourselves—redeemed us—we don't need to work unceasingly as if our salvation depends on it. God calls us not just to labor, but also to peace and joy. Life with leisure is a blessing of ongoing renewal even in the face of suffering. We can respond to God's call to leisure in at least four ways: contemplating God's love, resting in the peace of Jesus Christ, worshipping in spirit and truth, and living prayerfully.

Contemplating God's Love

My wife and I discovered during our sabbatical the value of *contemplation—giving attention to God's loving nature and good works*. We increasingly realized the gap between how society talks about God and how the Scriptures portray Jesus Christ. God is not available just when we have needs or are in a predicament. Instead God is active in his world, continually participating in loving acts of renewal.

In order to rediscover this reality, we had to escape temporarily from excessive busyness and intrusive noise. We needed to learn that God's loving presence sometimes is most evident when followers' minds are uncluttered and their hearts are free to behold the glory of Jesus Christ.

Nowadays contemplation seems archaic. Given all of the great communication technologies available, why would we want to embrace an old-fashioned practice like contemplation? After all, our friends, relatives, and co-workers want to hear from us. We have email and voice messages to answer. We can enjoy many TV channels, recordings, and websites.

The lack of interest in contemplation today ignores one over-riding truth: God has spoken and continues speaking. Genesis says that God uttered the world into existence. The mountains now sing the glory of God while the trees clap their hands.[1] Jesus Christ speaks through his own life on earth, as recorded in the Scriptures. The Gospel of John starts, "In the beginning was the Word." The Holy Spirit comforts us, encourages us in the faith, and urges us to be bold witnesses to the truth. Listening to God's Word, beholding his creation, and savoring his good works all enable us to know the Lord more fully.

As a form of attentive listening, contemplation has a *context* and a *center*. The *context* is shedding our minds of our own agendas so that we might attend to the Spirit's work. As some monasteries put it, "Speak only if you can improve upon the silence." The *center* is a heart of gratitude to God.

An acquaintance recently told me that she regularly strolls outdoors, giving attention to the clouds, plants, and animals. She finds herself witnessing things in nature that she otherwise does not notice, such as the shapes, shades, and textures of clouds. She also mentioned that she feels somewhat like a carefree child during these excursions, rediscovering the simple joy of taken-for-granted experiences. She cannot help but remember that the creation and salvation are gifts from God. As a result, her heart fills with gratitude.

When we shed our minds of our own noisy hopes and fears, of all desires except for the love of God, we are free to rediscover that we are utterly dependent on a Lord who is at work among us and in us. Moreover, as we open ourselves to what God is accomplishing rather than frantically plowing ahead with our own projects, we recognize more fully how majestic God is, how thoroughly invested Jesus Christ is in the renewal of all things, and how utterly dependent we are on the Holy Spirit for wisdom and comfort.

Some people contemplate by reflecting on a short section of Scripture—even on a key word, such as *salvation*, *grace*, or *peace*. Others recall how God has blessed them in their lifetimes, perhaps focusing each day on one period, event, or relationship. Still others discover that slowly, meaningfully repeating particular prayers encourages contemplation. My wife and I found that carefully observing nature deepened our relationship with God, since the creation speaks of the Creator's remarkable power, glory, and majesty.

Most people find that solitude is necessary for contemplation. Some protect quiet times early in the morning or before retiring at night. Others go for hikes on the weekends.

Regardless of how we approach contemplation, the purpose is to get a better bearing on the reality of God's love. We can contemplate such love on all levels, including the *intellectual* (the remarkable depth and complexity of God's creation), the *aesthetic* (the beauty of God's world and many things crafted by God's children), and the *affective* (the sheer joy and delight of being alive, living in loving relationships, and being a redeemed child of the risen Lord).

My contemplation in Florida brought to mind and heart these major reasons for my gratitude: God ultimately created me, gave me friends and family, provided employment and hobbies, put a roof over my family's head and food on our table, and blessed my family with a wonderful faith community. God's creation is stunningly beautiful, reflecting goodness in everything from blue herons to clouds. God's renewal of all things is under way. The wisdom of God's Word is profoundly trustworthy. Jesus Christ emptied himself on my behalf, giving me and other believers hope beyond measure. My congregation is one part of a body of Christ that extends around the globe and is growing in spite of persecutors' attempts to destroy it. Most important of all: Christ has died; Christ is risen; Christ will come again.

Contemplating God's love is a blessing that orients us to ultimate reality. It is one way of opening our hearts to divine generosity and thereby remembering why we should care for and about God's world. In addition to inspiring us to responsible caretaking, contemplation can direct us to a deeper rest in Jesus Christ.

Resting in Peace

Rest is a tremendous blessing if we accept it in the right spirit. A friend who grew up in a close-knit Christian community chuckles about his parents' rules for the Lord's Day. Reading a Sunday-school lesson and a Christian magazine took precedence over other reading. Play had to be fun, not work. Running around with friends was okay, but riding a bike was prohibited. No TV. No movies. Restaurants and stores were off-limits. Resting was a serious business!

My approach to the Lord's Day was less confining. As a college student, for instance, I studied at the library. The Sabbath was meant for man, not man for the Sabbath, I recalled from Scripture. In my view, the church was evolving toward a more enlightened view of the Lord's Day, which should include a bit of worship, lots of fun, and work. As the Bible puts it, when your ox falls into a well, you should immediately pull it out.[2] Work needs to get done. After all, medical staff, police, and cooks work on Sunday. So should I. Life must go on.

Unfortunately, my view of the Lord's Day was no better than that of my friend's parents. His kin often overemphasized communal restrictions. I focused way too much on personal freedom rather than healthy rest.

Lord's Day rest is one way of living in the peace of Jesus Christ. The God-given purpose of such rest is not to *prohibit* work as much as to *accept* grace. Jesus compassionately calls troubled and burned-out people to be comforted in his grace, where the burden is light.[3]

Thanks to Jesus's sacrifice on the cross, we caretakers don't have to try to justify ourselves by living legalistically. The Creator's own actions show us that life is intended to be joyful service and comforting rest, not enslaving work or debilitating anxiety.

After making the creation "very good," God sets aside time to enjoy it.[4] The Creator even blesses this first day of rest and begins a leisure-and-work rhythm that takes root in Hebrew culture in the Ten Commandments: "Six days you shall labor," instructs God. The seventh day is for rest.[5] This Sabbath rest is not meant merely to *balance* work and rest but to renew our whole lives *in* eternal rest. God's grace frees us from the burden of saving ourselves. Sabbath on earth is a foretaste of eternal rest, whether we practice it on Sunday or other days. Every believer enters this rest, but few of us savor it.[6]

Without rest, work slips into hellish idolatry, no matter how great the financial or social-status rewards. When we labor unceasingly, whether for pay or as a volunteer, we fail to acknowledge that we ultimately depend on God for all good things. God created the heavens and earth—we didn't. God saves us—we cannot save ourselves. We are called not just to new occupational stations, but also to "re-new" what God has already made. Rest gives us an opportunity to recognize and enjoy this gift of God-provided delight. Otherwise we get so enslaved by our own schedules and plans that our work torments us, day and night. We need pills or alcohol to sleep, caffeine to wake up, therapy to get someone to listen to us. We barely have time to care for ourselves, let alone for others.

Many of my current students jump from one assignment deadline to the next one, with barely a moment to remember God's easy burden. They went through high school with a to-do list. At college they upgraded to a day planner with more time slots. After college they often start computerized scheduling that allows others to access and even control their schedules. Eventually they discover that they are running from meeting to meeting nearly all day long. Lunchtime is for catching up on email and telephone messages. Cell phones and Internet connectivity keep them tied to work even when they are supposed to be on vacation. Work escalates in spite of time-saving technologies. Weekends are barely better.

Jesus, the "Lord of the Sabbath," challenges all such slavishness. He fulfills God's law and "sets us free" to live responsibly within liberty.[7] The Lord teaches that the Sabbath is not to be rejected, but lived rightly, in grace. We can do all kinds of things on the Lord's Day. We might dine with others, enjoy fellowship, and play in order to rediscover the peace of life in Christ.

Nevertheless, during our Sabbath rest, we ought to avoid non-stop work undertaken for personal gain. The fact that so many people around the world must work continuously just to make ends meet is tragic, since such incessant labor can deprive them of the joy of spiritual as well as physical rest. Accepting the gift of rest is a fitting way of *beginning* a new week in grace.

From a biblical perspective, rest is far more than another means to greater work efficiency or to mere recovery from labor. Rest is necessary for faithful following and journeying with Christ. We rest so that we are able to taste, enjoy, and celebrate the peace of Jesus Christ. But we also rest so that we can work more humanely, with a clearer focus on grateful caretaking rather than our own desires.

Sometimes it's hard to enjoy rest when we face many necessary tasks. Because of the broken world, we will have to work extra hard for periods. Sooner or later, however, we had better return to the rest-work rhythm or our diminished spiritual, emotional, and physical health will force us to do so. Life without Sabbath is secular, human centered, work driven, and spiritually impoverished. Life with rest is a taste of heaven on earth that renews our hearts and minds and prepares us for worship.

Worshipping in Spirit and Truth

Leisure also promotes fitting worship. God created the "very good" universe as a magnificent work of art. Suffering from brokenness, however, creation and culture groan for renewal. Parts of the environment have been exploited. Our personal lives are messed up. So are our workplaces, churches, neighborhoods, and friendships. Chaos surrounds us and is in each of us.

Even so, God is redeeming people and renewing all things. Goodness emerges, often where we least expect it. A marriage is revived. A person is healed of sickness. A new job gives delight in serving others. Justice is won. Most amazing of all, humble people admit their brokenness, turn to God for salvation, and celebrate with a community of faith.

While on sabbatical, my wife and I frequently went to the Gulf coast for sunsets. Each one was singularly beautiful and impressive. We praised God night after night as the great fireball dropped majestically on the horizon. Cloudy days simply heightened our desire to return again on sunny ones. This miracle of sunset, like a splendid painting in the sky, stirred our hearts and prepared us to worship God with other believers.

The most fitting way to give thanks for redemption and renewal is to worship the Triune God. We praise God partly by worshipping with our whole being—from our hearts, in spirit and in truth. The Triune God's excellent works are all around us, in us, and for us. We share together the glorious caretaking of God, especially the sacrifice and resurrection of his Son. As a community of faith, we remind ourselves that God promises never to leave us.[8]

Formal worship is a dialogue with God. Normally the dialogue begins with a call to worship.[9] Worshippers also hear about God's law, remember their sin, and then celebrate the gospel. The community thankfully responds by singing praise. A member prays for insight into God's Word, which is read and explained in a sermon.[10] Participants gratefully offer gifts to God. Sometimes worshippers share sacraments. Members pray for the needs of the congregation, the community, the country, and the world.[11] Often worshippers affirm together their beliefs through song. God bids a blessing through the minister, and faithful followers reenter the King's world, convicted once again to be living sacrifices.[12] These elements of worship can vary from church to church, but nearly all congregations employ them in some form.

In such corporate worship, we dialogue with God as a community, not just as individuals. God says, "You are my people." We respond, "You are our God." The Scriptures describe our relationship with God as similar to the faithfulness of bride and groom.[13] We become true to God, who is already true to us. We are betrothed ("be-truthed") to our Lord. Although *we* do the worship, such worship is God taking care of us. So worship becomes a model for how a community of believers cares for and about each other and the rest of God's world. We learn to be living sacrifices, grateful workers, advocates of peace and justice, communicators of the Word, and caretakers under God rather than under our own authority.

One of the greatest confirmations of the role of the Holy Spirit in the world is the emergence of new worshipping communities. This movement of the Spirit is occurring in Chinese homes, Latin-American Pentecostal congregations, rural Methodist churches, and college dorms. In Florida, my wife and I worshipped at churches that represented a wide range of music and preaching. We didn't like the style of every service, but our preferences are unimportant. The relevant fact is that God is busy near and far, calling all creation to praise him and to participate in his caring renewal of all things.

Worship is an essential station for leisure. It requires that we back away from our daily labors in order to praise God for his works near and far, long ago, and in the promised future. If we don't worship God, we are liable to praise something or someone else, especially our own works or the creation itself. When we fail to heed the call to worship God, we will manufacture *idols* ("nothings") as if they were worthy of our time, attention, and devotion. This is partly why we normally worship corporately on the first day of the week, the day of Christ's resurrection. By worshipping in spirit and truth, we respond faithfully to God's promise to redeem us and renew the entire broken creation. We are then more likely to live prayerfully.

Living Prayerfully

In his first letter to the church in Thessalonica, Paul calls us to a seemingly impossible practice: pray continually.[14] King David similarly tells people to bless the Lord at all times.[15] These and other biblical directives indicate that prayer is an essential way of caring in everything we do.

Nowadays, we tend to reduce prayer to a tool. Our prayers become a self-help technology. Sometimes we even press the prayer buttons in order to satisfy our wants, whether they are legitimate or not.

C. S. Lewis suggests that there are two seemingly contradictory forms of prayer. One is prayer of *petition*, asking God to intercede in specific ways for our own lives or for particular needs of the wider world. The other kind of prayer is "Thy will be done," an *affirmation* of God's own wisdom in action. Lewis concludes that we have to pray to God in order to know which kind of prayer to offer!

Paul commands us to pray continuously, King David calls us to praise God at all times, and Lewis reminds us to petition as well as trust God. Yet there is no way that we can literally pray for all things, pray at all times, or even know whether to petition God or simply affirm his wise ways.

Nevertheless, all of life's circumstances, from joy to devastation, are opportunities for one or another form of prayer. Life without prayer is secular, limited to relationships among people. Life with prayer opens our hearts to God. Since God hears our prayers and calls us to pray, we ought to pray—even when we don't know exactly what to pray or how to do so except for examples from Scripture.[16]

The beginning of a life of prayer is opening up to God during especially appropriate times and at appropriate places, such as when we rise and go to sleep, before we eat, at funerals and baptisms, during worship, and when our friends, families, nations, and world are in special need.

It is considerably more difficult for most of us to take the next step of *living prayerfully*. This kind of journey "in prayer" requires that we care enough to do all things consciously in the presence of God. In other words, we live openly before God, giving up all of our ridiculous attempts to hide parts of our days and nights from our Savior. For a follower, life is an ongoing relationship with God.

Being prayerful in our stations helps us to attend to the presence of God in all of our caretaking. If we remind ourselves throughout the day that we are God's children, saved by the sacrifice of Jesus Christ, we will try to conduct ourselves in the knowledge that God is with us and for us.

We live prayerfully by remembering to pray in all types of situations, not just when we feel desperate for God's help or when we officially should pray. The context for Paul's call to continual prayer is helpful: "Be joyful always; pray continually; give thanks in all circumstances, for this is God's will for you in Christ Jesus." He then adds, "Do not put out the Spirit's fire."[17] In other words, prayer is being oriented to God's love and mercy. Knowing in our hearts that he cares, we affirm and petition God in all things.

Often we tell people that we will pray for them when we hear about their need for discernment, healing, or comfort. Of course we should promise to pray for others. Prayerful living, however, should lead us to pray presently as well: "Lord, have mercy on my friend." "Please bless my co-worker." "Thank you for a day like today." "Forgive me."

The Michigan campus where I teach is beautiful in every season. Since the Florida sabbatical, I have found myself frequently thanking God for the grounds and buildings—even in the winter as the falling snow lays a smooth white blanket over dormant lawns and gritty streets. If I get too busy with work, I forget this gift of place. When my life is more leisurely, open to the needs of others and the joy of grace, campus is a place of prayerful living.

Conclusion

Leisure is a calling waiting to be celebrated, enjoyed, and shared. In leisure we give thanks by contemplating God's loving nature and good works, resting from unnecessary work, worshipping God, and living prayerfully. We should pursue leisure because it is right and fitting, not because we expect a payoff.

Without adequate leisure, we lose our ability to be followers. We might even find ourselves living frenetically, unable to contemplate, rest, worship, or pray. Leisure is not just nonwork time. It is part of sane, holy, restful, and God-directed caretaking of ourselves as well as God's world. We cease our own work in order to open ourselves to the life-giving deeds of God and to respond gratefully.

Jesus's invitation to rest is vital to hear today. We pile task upon task, mistakenly convinced that the more we work and the greater our accomplishments, the better our lives will necessarily become. We get so busy that we think God needs us rather than seeing the truth that we need God. Many churches and schools compound our overwork, burning out individuals and diminishing their rest in God. Continuous busyness—even nonstop ministry—is an enemy of true spirituality.

My wife and I had the gift of a sabbatical to rediscover the value of leisure. Knowing that most occupations do not have such a gift, we accepted it gratefully. When we returned home, though, we quickly realized that we had to adjust our lifestyles in order to continue flourishing in leisure. So we began saying no to many relatively unimportant requests for our time, and we began saying yes to more leisure. Now when we start to overwork, we recall the afternoon-napping blue heron. We are grateful that God used a bird to help point us to a way of living under Jesus's light burden. Clearly we are better stewards of God's gifts as a result.

6

Flourishing in Communities

German theologian Dietrich Bonhoeffer wrote influential works such as *The Cost of Discipleship* and *Letters and Papers from Prison*. He grew up during the 1920s in a close-knit Berlin family and by age sixteen felt called to study religion. When the dictator Adolf Hitler came to power in the 1930s, Bonhoeffer was on his way to becoming a highly respected theologian.

Unlike most ministers in the state church, Bonhoeffer stood publicly against Nazism. On the radio, he criticized Germans for following an idolatrous "misleader." He condemned the state church for compromising with the Nazi government.

Then a nonstate "Confessing Church" called him to lead a secret seminary. Bonhoeffer accepted the invitation and moved into a house with twenty-five men.

While residing and teaching there, Bonhoeffer wrote *Life Together*, which describes elements of Christian community, including prayer, confession, worship, and work. He argues that such community is necessary for the church if it hopes to speak wisely in society.

Anchored in and nurtured by his tiny community, Bonhoeffer skillfully cared for the German people. He taught and preached biblical wisdom. He wrote letters to church leaders and influential citizens. He visited people in spiritual need. For him, the community of faith was a home base for serving society. By the time Hitler had Bonhoeffer executed, he had already written books and letters that still inspire followers to pay the "cost of discipleship."

As Bonhoeffer recognized, *community is a calling to serve, work, and rest with others*. We live in many types of communities—for example, professional, familial, neighborhood. Pursuing stations without also nurturing community is spiritually and practically foolish. Although some communities can be stifling, those that nurture the caring use of diverse gifts can serve congregation, profession, neighborhood, and society. Participating in communities opens our eyes and ears to worthy stations and helps us to live faithfully within them.

We flourish in communities in at least five ways: learning to think cosmically, identifying and addressing needs, practicing reciprocity rather than mere networking, listening to mentors while mentoring others, and respecting work, family, and faith communities.

Thinking Cosmically

Living in Christian community helps us to think cosmically by taking on the mind of Christ.[1] Studying, worshipping, fellowshipping, and praying with other followers equip us to see the world biblically instead of merely from our own perspective. *Cosmic thought is anchored in God's order and wisdom rather than our own knowledge.*

In the beginning, God created an ordered *cosmos* out of the formless void,[2] establishing a world that was intrinsically good.[3] That cosmos included a perfect role for human beings as responsible caretakers under their Creator. Since the fall from grace, however, human beings have been reverting cosmos back to tangled chaos. History shows that people break relationships with each other, God, and nature. Their personal and shared lives lack the perfect order of the original creation.

In the face of such chaos, God calls us to participate in his just, peaceable order. This cosmic order—what the biblical writers called *shalom*—is both the absence of brokenness and the flourishing of peaceful relationships filled with joy and delight. Such relationships include those between God and people, among people, between people and the physical world, and each person's relationship with himself or herself.

Cosmic thinking helps us to anchor work and play in faith, thereby relating our vocation as responsible caretakers to our specific stations. It assumes that Scripture is, first, the story of God's saving grace and, second, our primary source of wisdom about how we should relate to God, others, nature, and ourselves.

For example, Bonhoeffer's Confessing Church strove to think cosmically about Hitler's message of totalitarianism and racism. While many state churches assented to racism, even using the Bible to justify it, Bonhoeffer's faith community fed on God's Word instead. As a result, the Confessing Church became an island of antiracist, justice-directed truth amidst the rising tide of anti-Semitism.

When St. Augustine became a priest and then a bishop in northern Africa, he faced the problem of conflicting biblical interpretations and doctrines—an issue that Christians confront in every era. His solution was profoundly simple yet deeply trusting of the Holy Spirit. God speaks, he argued, primarily through the body of believers, not via the whims of individuals. Persons might gain remarkable insights into God's Word, but even distinguished biblical scholars and revered preachers need to assess their ideas in the light of shared biblical wisdom.

Participating fully in Christian community, where both the Spirit and spiritual friends are present, is our primary means of learning how to be faithful caretakers. An acquaintance has pioneered ways that churches can find worthwhile employment for those released from prison. Another acquaintance has discovered that he can serve workers at his plant by offering free English-language training, leadership workshops, even personal money-management skills. These innovative practices emerged from engagement in faith communities, not merely from the individuals' own brainstorming.

We all can generate interesting ideas, but none of us can create them out of the blue. The Scriptures use the word *create* to refer only to what God does, not to what human beings do. Nor can we refine and implement ideas without others' assistance. Common conceptions about totally creative bohemian artists and revolutionary CEOs are largely modern-day mythologies. There is far less creativity in the world than we moderns tend to think. In fact, we might be losing more wisdom than we are gaining.

We learn how to care within our stations partly by becoming caretakers with other followers of Jesus Christ. Christian community in all of its forms can incubate biblical ideas and perspectives. C. S. Lewis, J. R. R. Tolkien, and other British writers met regularly in a pub to discuss their faith and work. They didn't always agree about how to approach their craft through the lens of faith, but their minicommunity nurtured fine literary works infused with Christian imagination.

As theologian Cornelius Plantinga Jr. suggests, occupations are most valuable to the kingdom of God when followers reform them for the good of society. In the broken world, cosmic thinking challenges or affirms the status quo with wisdom and discernment. But rarely does such discernment come purely from individuals; Jesus calls us to work with others, pray together, and hold each other accountable. "Deliver us from evil," says the Lord's Prayer. The New Testament word for church (*ekklēsia*) refers to an assembly of those who are called. Christ is present wherever two or more are gathered in his name. We are called to participate with others in Christ's renewal of all things.

In order to care *in* the world, we must learn to take on both the heart and mind of Christ, transforming brokenness into God's good order.[4] Usually we begin to strive for cosmic thinking when faced with actual problems that cry out for solutions.

Identifying and Addressing Needs

Communities help us to identify and address needs in the broken cosmos. It is especially easy for residents of wealthy countries to focus on serving people's general *wants* rather than striving to meet particular persons' or institutions' *needs*. Although it can be tough to distinguish between a want and a need—consider automatic transmissions for cars—community can help us to do so with greater accountability, sincerity, and empathy. Dwelling in a community, becoming a vital part of its identity and memory, better enables us to care skillfully for and compassionately about particular institutions and individuals. Parish, neighborhood, campus, township, and city present opportunities to identify and address needs. So do national and international associations, Christian denominations, cross-cultural friendships, and extended families.

"Place" is critically important for caring. Writer Frederick Buechner says that "the place God calls you to is where your deep gladness and the world's deep hunger meet." Although personal gladness is not without stress and suffering, our deepest satisfaction results from faithfully serving others in their brokenness.

We discover such gladness as we reach out to those who hunger for jobs, housing, education, medical care, and a voice in civic affairs. We might also find joy in fixing broken roads, producing worthwhile TV programming, leading worship services well, selling a good product at a fair price, or making our home a nurturing environment for neighborhood children.

A local church, for example, can help us identify the needs of the sick and dying; enlighten us about others' needs for security, hope, and faithfulness; and enable us to reach out to persons who need companionship, forgiveness, God, shelter, and prayer. A faith community should be one place where we discover some of the specific needs of our neighborhood, village, city, and world.

Of course, we can identify needs simply by following news reports and paying attention to the areas near where we work, worship, attend school, or play. Participating in a community, however, puts personal faces on needs even if they are expressed by visitors from afar. We then are less likely to be flighty tourists in God's world, but instead people who know, pray for, and work on behalf of specific institutions and persons.

A few years ago, my congregation began calling on people who lived across the street from our building. We discovered in low-income apartments many needy people, including adults who were unable to speak English and therefore could not apply for most jobs, children who required after-school tutoring so they could eventually pursue a greater number of opportunities in society, and families that lacked even food. Members of my

congregation worked together to address these needs by offering language training in our building, launching an after-school
tutoring program, initiating a community Bible study, and col-
laborating with a ministry that regularly delivers a truckload of
food. These projects required congregational prayer, neighborly
visits, committee planning, volunteer organizing, congregational
support, and many more community-essential activities.

Not all human needs are nearby, but even the needs that are
most distant are best addressed by those who dwell among the
needy. We should support missionaries, development workers,
and foreign relief agencies because they are most attuned to real
needs in actual places. But sending our financial contributions
to such caretakers and praying for them are insufficient for
genuine caring. We also need to hear their stories, the stories
of those for whom they care, and stories of how God is serving
both of them. Then we might learn what else we can do and how
we can live our own lives to serve marginalized communities
far away. Ignorance suffocates care, whereas knowledge opens
up opportunities to give and receive care.

My faith community also partnered with a congregation in El
Salvador. As members of my congregation researched the problems faced by Latin-Americans, many members felt called to do
more than blindly send money and missionaries to the region.
Thinking cosmically in discussions with our sister church, we
in the United States assisted prayerfully with resources and skill
as we had been blessed. We sent fellowship and training teams
to help with educational and medical programs that reached
from the church to the surrounding community.

In addition, my church realized that partnership is two-way
service. The Salvadorans could bless us, just as we could bless
them. We discovered in visits between the two congregations
that we had much to learn from our sister church about being
a *community* of faith. The Salvadorans showed us our own need
for deeper brotherhood and sisterhood.

A human community, including a church, is not merely a
collection of individuals but the most caring way of living with
and for others. We can discover in community both the needs of
the world and the kind of selflessness that points to our eternal
home in the New Jerusalem. We dwell with others, sharing the

joy of service, advocating peace and justice, and doing so as Christ's caretakers on earth.

Fostering Work Reciprocity

Work-related reciprocity—giving and receiving care among co-workers—nurtures mutual collegiality rather than selfish networking. Without reciprocity, networking leads to professional relationships that are merely tools for landing jobs, getting promotions, or transferring to better departments. As communities of reciprocity, however, professions can foster mutually beneficial relationships in which colleagues are respected, encouraged, and challenged to care. Such communities implicitly define persons not as mere workers, but as creatures with gifts for serving others.

Many books and workshops implicitly define networking too narrowly. "Who you know is more important than what you know," experts proclaim. Some students even attend elite colleges or universities primarily to get plugged into a network of successful alumni. Career-minded professionals might attend professional meetings or join professional associations primarily to advance their careers.

The concept of "career" itself tends to be individualistic, self-serving, and even secular. A *careerist* is interested primarily in personal success, not in mutual care. She or he typically seeks riches or prestige regardless of the cost to family, church, community, and other workers. In fact, the word "career" originally meant "race" or "racetrack." A careerist rushes wildly ahead without paying attention to anything occurring off the track. Like a horse wearing blinders, the careerist perceives little more than the finish line and the rear ends of any horses up ahead.

Since God desires that we care for and about others, selfish forms of networking are not the most fitting ways of building professional community. Theologian Eugene H. Peterson writes, "If the self exploits other selves, whether God or neighbor, subordinating them to its compulsions, it becomes pinched and twisted." We are called to avoid such brokenness by serving others through our professional skills and connections. In fact, the concept of "profession" comes from religion. Christians rightly talk about the importance of *professing* one's faith.[5] For the Christian, to be a work professional is to be a follower of Jesus within one's labor, thereby caring with excellence and compassion.

Work reciprocity is founded on the Golden Rule to treat others as we wish to be treated.[6] Living reciprocally, we will address our associates as if they were us. We will not be motivated by the desire to take from others, but instead by the desire to give and receive in thanks. We gratefully "give back" to our Redeemer by serving others as they serve us. There are at least four ways that we can foster such reciprocity.

We can express gratitude to associates. Most people are rarely thanked for their efforts. This is just as true for pastors as it is for postal carriers, stock traders, public officials, and speech pathologists. Students rarely thank their teachers, just as instructors fail to show gratitude to their pupils. Interns infrequently express appreciation to their supervisors or the instructors who arranged the opportunities. On and on goes this cycle of taking others for granted. One way to start practicing reciprocity is to spend a few minutes each day contemplating how God has blessed us through the words or deeds of colleagues and then to thank them sincerely.

We can pray for co-workers. This is an incredible gift. Because of Jesus Christ's work on *our* behalf, we can commune with God on behalf of *anyone.*[7] We have the right to petition God to care for and about them. Paul asks the Roman church to pray for him, knowing that those prayers will not be futile.[8] Even if we are initially too embarrassed or uncomfortable to inquire about others' needs, we can offer general prayers on their behalf.

We can introduce others to our colleagues. We all know people who might be willing to help others as well as us. Our family and friends alone represent a wide array of professional experience, skills, and knowledge. Why not ask our co-workers if they would be willing to aid others? If both parties are open to such introductions, and if they practice reciprocity, we ought to facilitate such relationships.

We can offer others our own knowledge, skills, and wisdom. We might do this naturally at professional meetings, workshops, and conferences. But we also can give according to the needs that we discover among friends, family, interns, and co-workers. I have opportunities to share with my students some of my knowledge about graduate school, consulting, writing skills, and wisdom about mentoring. I also discover situations in which I can help others save time and money, avoid unethical conduct, and work for the renewal of indifferent or oppressive social institutions.

Although all four practices foster community in stations, these practices also can be badly distorted. We should beware of individuals who seek merely to use us for their own ends. We also should pay attention to our own needs so we don't burn out from giving without receiving.

Apart from such warnings, reciprocity is far superior to mere networking. Reciprocity is one form of mutual caretaking that tunes us in to others' needs, cultivates community, provides opportunities for mutual caring, and spreads the Golden Rule.

Listening to Mentors and Mentoring Others

One of the richest forms of professional or personal community is *mentoring—trustworthy, one-on-one advising about work and life*.

When I was a public university student, an instructor made fun of Christianity during a class session. He also gave me the lowest grades I had ever received. I worried that I might fail his course and be dropped from my program. Suffering from fear and anxiety, I could not think clearly.

Then I acted foolishly. In order to determine if this instructor was biased, I submitted a paper that a peer had used in the same course a few years earlier. My friend had received an outstanding grade, whereas I earned only a very poor one. The result confirmed my suspicions. To make matters even worse, I felt horribly guilty for acting so unwisely. This was my low point in college. I was forced to face the fact that I was impulsive rather than careful.

I prayed for insight, consulted with my fiancée, and sought a mentor for advice. Normally a mentor provides ongoing advice rather than just a rescue, but the person I chose was already a trustworthy friend and respected professor. After hearing my story and consenting to help me, he went to the offending instructor on my behalf and worked out a compromise that required me to do additional work in the class but also ensured that I would be graded fairly.

My mentor taught me not to overly rely on my own judgment, particularly in tough situations. I began to see that in each of life's stations, from marriage to work to friendship, we all need the help of a more experienced person.

Good mentors are rightly held in AWE. They offer *accountability*, *wisdom*, and especially *experience*. Fine mentors hold themselves to high standards of excellence and compassion. They share practical knowledge as well as wisdom. Mentees should listen carefully to such mentors.

The best way to locate a mentor is by initiating reciprocity with admired persons in one's own faith community. Offer to take one to breakfast or lunch. If we cannot find a solid Christian mentor, we should turn to someone who embodies Christian values, acts with a deep conscience, and respects our faith commitments.

We know in our hearts when we find the right mentor. Usually we won't even have to officially ask the person to be a mentor. Mentoring usually emerges as a minicommunity when reciprocity is present.

Each of us will discover opportunities to mentor others. A high school senior might serve ably as a mentor to freshmen or younger siblings. An experienced pastor could be called to shepherd seminary students. An accomplished psychologist might mentor a beginner. Mentoring provides a vital succession of accountability, wisdom, and experience.

God works through faithful mentoring, producing unexpected and even glorious results. Years later, the instructor who criticized Christianity and tried to fail me became a believer. I thank God that my mentor protected me from being an even bigger fool. Otherwise I might have been a stumbling block to the budding faith of a professor.

Respecting Work, Family, and Church

Wise mentors rightly caution us about letting work consume our lives. Work is only one station, a single source of obligations and joys. We all have and need other stations, especially family and church. If we truly respect our family, we will dedicate the time and love necessary for it to flourish. Few marriages and faith communities thrive amidst workaholism.

Families need intentional nurturing. In some Christian traditions, the family is the primary community. In others, the family and church are equally significant. In either case, the family draws some of its social and spiritual strength from a faith community while contributing reciprocally to the congregation. Meanwhile, an active church life equips us to be faithful rather than merely successful in our occupational stations.

Christians inherit the freedom in Christ to think creatively about how to respect work, family, and church. Some couples respect all these areas through job-sharing with other workers. A growing number of spouses put one of their careers on hold at a time so a spouse can be the primary caretaker at home. Yet others seek jobs that permit telecommuting or independent contracting for more flexible schedules. One friend contracts with a firm that allows her to specify how many projects she undertakes each quarter. A few churches provide child care, arrange household groups that share homeschooling duties and babysitting, and provide community assistance to parents who need their children picked up from school.

Singlehood has its own challenges, especially in defining family life. Clearly singlehood itself is a worthy calling, but some churches and married friends don't serve singles as well as they do families. In order to avoid being consumed by their work or ignored by their congregation, singles need to cultivate an extended family in the church.

Families flourish when members care enough to say no to some work in order to say yes to relationships. Sometimes this requires professional sacrifice, but it always depends on respect for family, church, and work. Even Billy Graham, the best-known and most-admired American evangelist of the second half of the twentieth century, admitted late in his life that he regretted not spending more time with his children and grandchildren.

Conclusion

My son called from a graduate school he was thinking about attending. We discussed the advantages and disadvantages of that university, its academic programs, and the surrounding community. Neither of us felt any clear sense of God's direction for him. Then he spoke words of wisdom: "Dad, I just don't think I could flourish here." We dropped that school from his list.

God wants us to flourish. In this broken world, we might grieve or suffer for being faithful caretakers. We might even be called to challenge corporate decisions or turn down a job that would require us to neglect our family or act contrary to our faith. But when we live in community, we don't have to journey alone. We travel with other followers, offering mutual encouragement and consolation. Participating in good communities, we are more likely to have the courage to be faithful caretakers. Just knowing that others care for and about us helps our spirits flourish even during tough times. Mary had Elizabeth as well as Joseph. The Lord invites us to journey with others for encouragement, companionship, and growth in faith.

The psalmist describes such flourishing as an olive tree nurtured by God's unfailing love.[9] Followers of Jesus Christ grow well when they live in right relationships that honor God and serve others. Occupational success is a bonus but not alone adequate for flourishing. When their professional relationships fall apart, Christians too discover how much they need to journey with other caretakers.

Today many people's mobility and busyness make it increasingly hard to cultivate faith communities. For some believers, "going to church" means little more than weekly worship with strangers. Some Christians don't even feel comfortable turning to other believers when they face trials. An acquaintance told me that Alcoholics Anonymous serves as a better community for her than does her local congregation, which is quick to judge and slow to care. Sadly, her community of faith is not accepting of broken people.

God calls us to communities. Bonhoeffer responded faithfully, creating an underground seminary and serving his country courageously as an agent of renewal. Communities can help us to think cosmically, address real needs, form reciprocal work relationships, equip us to mentor and be mentored, and help us to flourish in church and family as well as work.

7

Loving for Good

I grew up in a highly dysfunctional family. My father and mother argued daily, sometimes violently. They seemed to be more interested in hurting each other than caring for me.

After they died and I matured, I began to understand that my parents could not care for me very well because they were coping with occupational failure, marital breakup, and debilitating diseases. Although my mother and father struggled to love others, they sank into the quicksand of mutual condemnation, cutting themselves off from support communities and failing to care even for themselves.

Blaming rather than loving is a recurring theme in the Scriptures. Adam criticizes Eve, who in turn faults the serpent for the couple's disobedience. Cain eventually kills his brother rather than dealing with his own lack of love for God and sibling.

Love is the chief virtue for caretaking, since it reflects the very character of the God who calls us to follow him. Love stretches us beyond our own interests to serve others. Good *character*—that is, a tendency to *be* a good person, not just *act* rightly—is evident whenever people demonstrate loving attitudes and actions.

The Bible emphasizes at least three ways we can concretely love others: *nurturing friendship*, or sacrificing for those we know; *offering hospitality*, or making room in our minds, hearts, and homes for those who are different than us; and *being a good neighbor*, or assisting anyone in need.

Friendship—Sacrificing for Those We Know

Shortly after I was born, my parents faced major crises. My mother contracted tuberculosis and was confined for more than a year to a hospital. She and my father sent me to live with an aunt. My father struggled to make a living while raising his other two sons, eventually losing the battle to alcohol. Meanwhile, my mother could not cope with being separated from her family. She became increasingly paranoid and eventually schizophrenic, a condition that plagued her for the rest of her life.

By the time my mother's tuberculosis was cured, my parents had become foes, blaming each other for their setbacks. My mother branded my father a "drunk," while my father labeled her a "psycho." Eventually they separated, divorced, and died. They were never able to revive their friendship, let alone their marriage.

Friendship is an essential station. It is relatively easy to form acquaintances, but true friendship is a more satisfying, longer-term relationship. *Biblically speaking, friendship is sacrificial caring between persons who know each other's needs.*

Although there are different levels of friendship, the Bible defines it as persons bound together in self-sacrifice. Jesus says, "Love each other as I have loved you." The greatest love, the deepest friendship, is laying down one's life for a friend.[1]

Self-sacrifice is vital for friendship. A friend loves so deeply that she might sacrifice a career on the other's behalf or even take the place of the other in prison. This biblical ideal is uncommon in the real world, but we should yearn and strive for it. Even a moderately deep friendship is a sign of Christ's own friendship with us.

In this broken world, however, most of our friendships are superficial. We tend to form and dissolve them without long-term commitments. At work, we network rather than reciprocate. We attend church instead of participating in deeper fellowship. We treat college or other roommates as short-term acquaintances, content merely to get along with them.

Families, which should provide some of the strongest friendships, are often fractured as well. Many marriages lack deep mutuality. Adult siblings can become enemies over issues such as inheritances, politics, and whom to marry. Cross-generational friendships, especially between parents and their children, tend to be weak in industrial societies.

We struggle to form friendships partly because dreamy relationships are society's primary role models for emotional closeness. Male-female friendships are especially hard because there is so little social space for emotionally deep but nonphysical relationships. On many Christian college campuses, students have only two alternatives—either to maintain an identity as a single person by participating in relationally superficial groups, or to be deemed "engaged" just by being seen a few times with the same person.

We also fail to form genuine friendships because we fear transparency. We conceal our hearts in order to save face and avoid possible rejection. Friendship makes us vulnerable because others will discover our failings as well as our triumphs, our doubts in addition to our faith.

Finally, we neglect friendships in our busyness. Sometimes we assume that we can form friendships later in life, once we are professionally triumphant. It doesn't always occur to us that we might alienate budding friends along the way.

One of my former friends ignored her family as she strove for social status. Today she is a lonely hypochondriac who dwells in an expensive condo. She attends fancy dinners but lacks real fellowship. Worst of all, she blames her situation on family and former friends—the very people she dismissed during her compulsive climb up the ladder to high society.

There are two crucially important ways of nurturing friendship. First, potential friends engage in relational activities, such as meeting for conversation, going for walks, volunteering, and traveling together. Second, friends listen to their respective life stories. In these two friendship-oriented activities, we become like Christ, available for fellowship and eager to listen. Jesus's friendship with us is our model for earthly friendships.

Hospitality—Making Room for Strangers

Sometimes hospitality is the beginning of friendship. In any case, hospitality is much more than hosting friends in our homes. *Hospitality is the practice of "making room" in our own heart, mind, and home for the stranger among us.*

The radical concept of hospitality comes from the ancient world. Throughout history, hospitable persons, families, and tribes hosted people from different cultures, social classes, and ethnicities.[2] Hospitality was a socially important practice for the good of both the host and the stranger. The benefits of such hospitality included reduced stereotypes, fewer ethnic and cultural conflicts, and cross-cultural friendships. Peace among tribes depended partly on the practice of hospitality.

Given all of the crime and conflict in some cities today, hospitality seems unsafe. We are much more comfortable inviting only our friends and associates to our homes, interacting exclusively with those who are like us.

In contrast, the New Testament teaches that followers are called to practice hospitality for the stranger.[3] Being hospitable is as important as practicing sincerity, clinging to what is good, and praying faithfully.[4] This radical form of hospitality is a good way of caring for others on God's behalf. Jesus even says that being hospitable to people is like inviting the Lord into our lives.[5] God makes clear that a follower is called to treat strangers honorably, as if they are the Lord.

The potential dangers involved in hosting strangers are offset by likely gains. When the angel-messengers visit Abraham, the faithful Israelite offers his home to three strangers, serves a meal, and engages in conversation.[6] He could have been robbed or even killed. Instead, God communicated his will through Abraham's hospitality. The Israelite's relatively simple yet dangerous actions became vital steps in the redemption of God's people.

Because of the uncertain results of hospitality, the host might be taken advantage of or even put friends and family in jeopardy. Certainly we should consider the risks and ensure reasonable safety. For instance, inviting friends to cohost strangers is sensible. But avoiding all risk reduces hospitality to thoroughly comfortable interactions with those who are like us.

Among the most important forms of hospitality today are civic, church, and college programs aimed at cross-cultural understanding. Many schools, for instance, offer student-exchange programs, off-campus semesters, and service-learning opportunities in the broader community. For example, our daughter spent a semester in Spain, living with a native woman, studying at a college, and attending a local church.

When we open our homes, minds, and hearts to strangers, we often challenge our tidy, simplistic understandings of reality. We deepen our appreciation for other persons, unfamiliar cultures, and even God. We are likely to learn that God is far greater than what we had imagined and that God's love transcends our meager knowledge and limited experience. Hosts and guests can be mutually encouraged, be enlightened about cultural differences, and grow more thankful.

The results of opening up to strangers and even enemies can be miraculous. John Perkins, an African-American pastor whose brother was killed by a white police officer, became a brother in Christ to Thomas Tarrants, a former member of the white-supremacist Ku Klux Klan. After Perkins and Tarrants first met, they began sharing their own life stories as well as their common faith in God. By grace, these individuals hosted each other across the nation's racial divide. Eventually they even coauthored *He's My Brother: Former Racial Foes Give a Strategy for Reconciliation*.

My wife and I were convicted of the power of hospitality while in Guatemala City, where we were invited to dine with a woman and her two young children in their ramshackle hut. Visiting the area to conduct research, we were surprised by the invitation. We thought that we should decline because our hosts barely had enough to feed their own families. Many of the residents in this area scrounged for food in the nearby garbage dump. But friends who lived in Guatemala informed us that to turn down an invitation would be an insult. So we graciously accepted.

In order to serve us at her simple table, the woman gave her daughter some empty glass bottles to trade for eggs and tomatoes. When the daughter returned with the provisions, her mother scrambled the eggs on a small griddle over a fire in a living room corner that was open to the sky. The food was delicious and the conversation stimulating. We exchanged stories about Christianity in the United States and Guatemala, since this was a small family of believers.

During the meal, my wife and I realized that these materially poor people were exceptionally kind and generous hosts. We experienced the love of Christ in their home, yet we also recognized that such selfless hospitality frequently was lacking back home in our relatively affluent community. We were embarrassed, even ashamed about our inhospitality. We concluded that we were more interested in being comfortable than in comforting strangers. Our Guatemalan hosts were Christlike caretakers whose actions called my wife and me to practice similar hospitality back home.

Our reflections on hospitality brought to mind Jesus's dinner at the house of a prominent religious leader. Noticing that the well-to-do guests had taken the places of honor at the table, Jesus tells a parable about a wedding feast where self-important people grabbed the most prestigious places, only to be humiliated when even more distinguished guests arrived to take those spots. Each exalted person "will be humbled," says Christ, and each humbled person "will be exalted."

Then Jesus adds that hosts should not invite only family or influential people, but also the persons who have little power or prestige.[7] In other words, hospitality is designed to undermine corrupted power structures by bringing people together across social divisions. True hospitality reflects a renewed social order in the New Jerusalem.

Jesus shows that hospitality is a way of *witnessing* the love of Christ to all people. When we host strangers, we accept God's call to love others as he loves us. We too were strangers to God. By grace we have been brought back into God's family. Now our hospitable actions witness to the love of Christ. Jesus, the host, invites *his* broken people to *his* banquet table, where we celebrate eternal life as *his* guests.

People who practice true hospitality accept and honor the stranger as if welcoming Jesus Christ.[8] Each time we love the stranger, we give her or him an opportunity to sample the unconditional love that defines Jesus's own sacrifice on the cross. We open our hearts, minds, and homes to serve refreshment and fellowship—signposts that point to the eternal hospitality of the greatest of all caretakers, Jesus Christ.

Neighborliness—Helping All in Need

In one sense, neighborliness is our primary vocation as caretakers. Friendship and hospitality are ways of being good neighbors to those we know well (friends) and those we don't (strangers).

But there is also a more nuanced sense of neighborliness. According to Scripture, neighborliness is more inclusive. *A good neighbor selflessly assists anyone in need.*

Motive is critically important in neighborly love. We ought to help others not because we seek something in return, but only because they are in need. Called by God to assist them, we care for them as we would want to be treated in a similar situation. Being a good neighbor is a way of "getting out" of ourselves and serving someone else without prejudice.

When I was about ten years old, I was riding with my older brother through a forest preserve when we suddenly saw a car that had crashed into a tree. My brother immediately pulled over, grabbed a blanket from his trunk, and ran to the accident scene as others began arriving. A few minutes later, he returned to his vehicle without the blanket.

"What did you do?" I asked him.

"Look," he responded, "when you run across an accident, you stop to help. It's just the right thing to do."

"Was anybody hurt?"

"Yes, but the ambulance is on the way, and they have blankets to keep warm in the meantime."

I frequently recall how proud I was of my sibling and how scared I was about the crash. I remember wondering if people would have stopped to help us if we had been the victims.

All of us discover others who are in need. The chief question is whether we will try to help, not whether we will succeed.

Friends and I tried to help a young woman escape temporarily from an abusive marriage so that she could seek safety and help. In spite of our careful planning and loving approach, she would not accept the safety that we offered. Her abusive spouse, meanwhile, found out what we had done and cut us off from further contact with his wife. We had hoped for a better ending, but at least we did what we could to assist a woman in a horrible situation.

Sometimes it's hard to discern if we can really help or not, but usually our consciences offer a clue. I experienced this while getting a haircut at a beauty school in Iowa just before Christmas. I noticed a senior citizen hobbling into the shop out of the brutal cold. She wore several sweaters, a scraggly coat, a stocking cap, gloves, and cheap rubber boots. Since I was seated close to the front door, I could hear her chatting with the receptionist about needing a permanent. The receptionist quoted her a price, and the woman responded by slowly counting all of the money she could find in her purse.

Apparently the woman did not have sufficient cash, because she returned to the receptionist and asked if there was another option. I could not make out the answer, but I saw the receptionist shake her head. The woman stood there confused as the receptionist returned to her desk. I concluded that the heavily bundled woman probably was too poor to afford a perm even at an inexpensive school.

Suddenly I had the feeling that the woman was someone's mother. I even imagined *my* mother coming through the front door bewildered. I remembered that it was just before Christmas and that this woman—like my mother—might have been trying to prepare for a visit from her family. I felt badly as she stood in the doorway, lonely and confused. I did not pity her. I simply felt that she deserved better as a human being. Getting one's hair done at a beauty school is hardly a sign of excessive affluence or selfish pampering.

Moments later, when my haircut was finished, I paid the receptionist and gave her enough additional money to cover the woman's perm. "Please treat her well," I said and quickly left.

Neighborliness is part of the moral fabric of good, conscience-driven relationships among friends, within families, and between strangers. As in the parable of the good Samaritan, only one major question should influence our neighborliness: how can I give care to this person? Our actions should flow selflessly from this calling.

We rightly wonder about which of the many needs to address with our limited time, resources, and skills. We should consider when and where our neighborliness will truly serve others. For instance, we ought to ensure that an international relief organization will wisely use our contributions on behalf of people who most need help.

Nevertheless, effectiveness can be tough to discern. When I pass a panhandler on the street, I cannot know if the person will spend a gift on drugs, alcohol, food, or shelter. I have seen successful panhandlers immediately purchase food. And I have observed others run to the nearest liquor store. Some bless me even when I do not give them any money. And others curse me for not offering them any cash even when I don't have any. So what? We should act as good neighbors because we are followers of Jesus Christ, not because we expect to solve the world's problems even one at a time.

We are called to be the face of Jesus to those in need, not to judge our neighbors.[9] Loving God and neighbor are twin signs of our gratitude to Jesus Christ. As Jesus says, these two loves represent the fulfillment of the law.[10] They are more important than all self-serving offerings and sacrifices.[11]

Like hospitality, neighborliness points to peace and justice without distinctions of race, age, ethnicity, or religion. Both practices are based on the fact that the New Heaven and the New Earth will host many different tribes, tongues, and cultures.[12]

Seen in this light, neighborliness is risky love. Often we don't know the recipients or even whether we are safe in assisting them. Our offer to care might get us into trouble. Still, we are called to take some risks, however measured, because we are God's caretakers on earth. We are Jesus to neighbors during their time of need.

Although neighborliness is easier to offer to friends, the parable of the good Samaritan shows that we should practice it without bias even in the face of potential risks. Neighborliness defies human brokenness. It challenges selfishness, indifference, and arrogance. When followers journey as neighbors, they resist the social and cultural forces that separate human beings.

Conclusion

God's love is the ultimate standard for friendship, hospitality, and neighborliness. We cannot live up to Christ's measure of selflessness, but we can do whatever is in our power to put love into action. Virtuous love is intrinsically good and pleasing to God. "Dear friends," John writes, "let us love one another, for love comes from God. Everyone who loves has been born of God and knows God."[13]

Friendship, hospitality, and neighborliness are three Christ-like ways of caretaking in all of our stations. Paul says that each Christian is given the Holy Spirit "for the common good."[14] Whether at work or play, on the road or at the barber, in North America or Guatemala, we will find opportunities to sacrifice for friends, host strangers, and assist neighbors. Every time we act upon these opportunities, we bless others.

Sometimes I wish that my parents had lived longer so that I could have loved them more fully. I imagine offering them hospitality. I dream about being a friend who loves them more deeply than they cared for each other. Occasionally I even wonder what it would have been like to be a neighbor when my father was desperate for a drink or my mother was hopelessly conversing with nonexistent persons.

I suppose my wishes are not wrong. But I have to avoid taking upon myself the burden of loving them now in ways that I was incapable of doing when they were on earth. I know that I should release them to God. In fact, I should give to God all of my dreams about love. Like every person in God's good but broken world, my parents and I are invited to bathe in the love of Jesus Christ, who opens his arms to strangers, reaches out to neighbors, and has already sacrificed himself as a friend beyond measure.

8

Offering a Legacy

A few years ago, my wife and I attended her grandfather's funeral. The event attracted many friends and family to celebrate Grandpa John's 102 years on earth.

Wherever he went, John loved and was loved. He established lifelong business associates. Friends and strangers alike chatted with him during his daily walks; he took hospitality with him everywhere. Dozens of children swarmed around him before and after worship, enjoying his endless supply of peppermints, smiles, and pats on the head. John led weekly singing at a nursing home, even though he never resided there and most of the residents were younger than he was. He spent mornings at a doughnut shop, befriending the customers and the immigrant owners—perhaps because he was once a Dutch immigrant.

John was an extraordinarily faithful caretaker who celebrated life as he experienced God's grace. His kind demeanor and upbeat attitude reflected the love of Jesus Christ. Although he was far from perfect, in the long run he was faithful. To know him was to touch grace incarnate. His funeral reminded attendees to be like Christ, not just like Grandpa John.

Each of us is called to establish a commendable *legacy—a faithful witness to God's love that "speaks" to others long after*

91

we die. Whether we are new or experienced followers of Christ, our lives today will shape others' futures. Our demeanor and actions are like boats in the water, creating wakes that can throw others off course or equip them to navigate faithfully through a turbulent world. Three caring practices are critically important for cultivating commendable legacies: living gratefully, giving generously, and reflecting the face of Christ to others.

Living Gratefully

Perhaps the most influential element of our personal legacy is our attitude toward life. Even as we diligently care skillfully for and compassionately about others, our underlying attitude can project a corresponding or contrary message.

Each of us radiates an attitude somewhere along a continuum from thankfulness to ingratitude. People who grumble all the time, for instance, usually are unappreciative. They focus on their own problems and are quick to blame others, sometimes even God. Ungrateful people fault colleagues, friends, and loved ones but are slow to admit their own weaknesses. Paul says that one of the marks of rebellion against and alienation from God is a lack of gratitude.[1]

The broken world gives all of us plenty to grumble about. Nothing is perfect. Rarely will our career or other stations unfold according to our dreams. Even our closest friends can hurt us. We experience disappointments almost daily.

When we adopt an unconstructive outlook, however, we become part of the very problem we lament. We carry and spread bad news into our stations. The world then seems to conform to our own unhappiness.

During high school, I worked summers at a factory that provided a paid coffee break for employees. Every morning a group gathered for twenty minutes to talk about the news, sports, and work. Invariably the discussion sank into gossip about bosses and other workers. Participants seemed to enjoy making uncharitable comments, while I tried unsuccessfully to redirect the conversation. Since my own attitude toward co-workers was souring, I left that group and started a new one with more congenial people.

Grandpa John journeyed through much heartache, from losing his home during the Depression to seeing his wife die three decades before his 102nd birthday. During it all, however, his disappointments and grief did not determine his view of reality. He recognized that in the larger picture of God's grace, he was enormously blessed. For him, the travails of this world were relatively minor in contrast with the glory of eternal life in Christ. Without ignoring his earthly responsibilities, Grandpa John lived faithfully in the knowledge that all things eventually work together for good for those who love Jesus Christ.[2]

Friends, strangers, and neighbors witness our attitude about life. Moreover, our manner will tend to encourage or dishearten them. As we live out our attitude, we implicitly invite others to adopt the same stance. The impact can extend for generations.

Having been raised in a home where grumbling surpassed gratitude, I later realized that I had to deal with my own acquired negativity. I recall reading Jeremiah's frightening observation that the misdeeds of the parents are passed along to their children.[3] I realized that I was becoming increasingly like my unappreciative, argumentative mother and father who belittled each other daily. The more I thought about my own negative attitude, the greater my self-criticism! I was sinking into ungratefulness and despair, finding fault with everything and everyone, including myself.

Later I read in Hebrews that the cross of Jesus Christ now covers the failures of each follower in every generation.[4] In spite of our individual pasts, we can dwell in a fresh relationship with the God of love. Some of our previous troubles will still pull us down, but our brokenness is not the end of the story. In Christ, we are new creatures. The old self is dying, and the new self is already rising like a phoenix out of the ashes. We still need to act faithfully, but we shouldn't condemn ourselves for imperfection. Gratitude motivates a faithful caretaker.

Where there is new life, there are renewed people, other caretakers journeying with us on the road to deeper gratitude to God. The church, the body of Christ, dwells under the watchful eyes of God and will never be destroyed, even as our personal lives sometimes fall apart. Citing the book of Hebrews (12:28), the Radical Reformer Menno Simons (1496–1561) said that no persons or institutions will ever completely destroy the church.

The bottom line is that sadness, sickness, and conflict are temporary signs of brokenness, not reflections of eternal reality. We should grieve over loss, challenge injustice, and be peaceful caretakers amidst the world's many trials. Surely we also should speak the truth in love, even when it hurts. At the same time, Christ offers abundant reasons to rejoice no matter how severe our earthly losses. He saved us for eternal life. He loves the church as his bride and will continue to serve it. So we ought to avoid creating legacies of pessimism as if Christ is not our eternal Lord and Savior.

Living gratefully means being a carrier of the Good News even as the world and our own lives sometimes fall apart. In every stage of life, we face new challenges and seemingly irresolvable issues. Accepting this immediate brokenness is not easy, but it is possible by grace. Grandpa John lived this testimony for four generations. He worked hard and attended responsibly to many stations, but probably his most enduring legacy is his heart of gratitude in the midst of disappointments as well as joys. Now this caretaker's witness goes forward after his death, from person to person, like a love letter of thanks to God. Our legacy too will go forward even after we join the "great cloud of witnesses."[5]

Giving Generously

We also form Christlike legacies by giving generously. Every blessing we behold is meant to be accepted, appreciated, and then returned to God through grateful caretaking in all stations.

I chatted one day with a student who was volunteering at a house-based library ministry in the inner city. He and other students dedicated time each week to serve neighborhood kids who needed a safe place to learn and play. Intrigued by his enthusiasm for this ministry, I decided to visit.

There I discovered a multicultural group of children reading books, working on a computer, and listening to storytellers. The nun in charge and various volunteer college students were holding the hands of their young friends, sitting with them on the floor, being older brothers and sisters. The warmly decorated home clearly was a sign of hope in a community wracked by unemployment, despair, drug addiction, alcoholism, and broken families. I was filled with joy.

Before I left, my student expressed sadness about leaving town after graduation. "I have been a stable friend in the lives of some of these children," he admitted, "and I just hope that they will understand that I have to go." He then asked me to help find another student or two to take his place. It was the least I could do to honor this student's caretaking at the ministry, although by God's grace his legacy will continue anyway in the lives of those young people whom he served.

My student had learned the irreducible value of giving to others. Faithful giving is a commendable return on God's generous investment in us.

Christlike generosity is not easy to practice. Wise giving requires discernment as well as a generous heart. Our legacy in giving emerges from *what*, *how*, and *why* we give.

Often the people who own the least are the ones who give the most generously from their hearts. Students tell me that the biggest tippers at restaurants tend to be working-class people, not the wealthy. I have noticed while traveling that materially poor people often are most courteous and friendly.

At the same time, however, I have seen incredible generosity among affluent people. Some well-to-do persons even practice downward mobility. A highly respected businessperson in my community gave up a major inheritance in order to go into public service. He could have served God in either station, but he felt called to serve as a full-time community leader working on behalf of the less fortunate. Other persons invest their time and talents to generate wealth on behalf of their communities and churches, mission agencies, and worldwide relief efforts. Such people are critically important to many worthy endeavors.

The New Testament says that we all should practice wholehearted generosity because it is a fitting way of praising God and serving others. Our vocation as caretakers is to bless others with a generous spirit and deeds. We are called, for instance, to be rich in hospitality, friendship, and neighborliness.[6] The creation, the Holy Spirit, the sacrifice of Jesus Christ, and Jesus's second coming are spectacular, even miraculous, gifts.

In heartfelt thankfulness, we imitate God, who provides most generously for us.[7]

The biblical story of sisters Mary and Martha affirms the importance of wholehearted giving. Martha kindly opens her home to Jesus. Her sister, Mary, sits at Jesus's feet while Martha prepares the meal. Soon Martha grows angry and probably jealous. "Lord, don't you care that my sister has left me to do the work by myself? Tell her to help me!" Jesus acknowledges that Martha is "worried and upset about many things," but he also reminds Martha that "only one thing is needed. Mary has chosen what is better, and it will not be taken away from her."[8]

Mary's "better way" is giving Jesus her undivided attention and sincere devotion—not her lack of "work." Martha certainly seeks to present food to Jesus, but Mary offers God a relationship, her wholehearted devotion as well as her good works. Martha's efforts are wonderful as far as they go. But is she willing to worship in her work by thankfully praising God in each mealtime preparation? A grateful attitude of giving is just as important as the good works themselves.

God similarly wants us to love and thank him by being a blessing to others. Selfless, heartfelt giving is itself a way of praising God. A generous spirit naturally leads to the most charitable giving of time, skill, and wealth.

In wealthy societies, people mistakenly measure generosity by the quantity of cash that people contribute to worthy causes. They even talk about some givers' "deep pockets."

More important than such stereotypes is whether each of us is generous with *whatever God has granted us*. Most of us will go through financially difficult times when we can offer only time, expertise, and a listening heart. Our legacy includes *all* giving, even the "little things" that can be so important to recipients—a word of encouragement, a note of thanks, an invitation to dinner. A member of my congregation recently said that one of the greatest blessings she receives from the church is an opportunity to teach and love others' children, since she never had any.

As long as we keep our motive as pure as possible, we can properly accept God's blessings in return for our gifts to others. If we give primarily to make ourselves feel good or to impress others, our generosity is hardly virtuous. If we give from our heart, even if we cannot offer much materially, we will experience God's blessings. Proverbs tells us that givers prosper and are refreshed.[9] Paul adds that those who sow generously will reap abundantly.[10]

This reaping is not necessarily financial or even material. We might gain joy and delight—as my student found while serving inner-city youth. Or we might obtain peace. Probably the most satisfying reward is witnessing how God works to renew the broken world through our weakness as well as our strength.

Our giving spirit and deeds become influential legacies in each station. My wife and I discovered this with our children, who as toddlers began imitating our actions at church, home, and neighborhood gatherings. I saw the influence of legacy when, as a church elder, my good or bad leadership became a role model for the congregation as well as other elders. The wide-ranging influence of professional legacy gripped me when I became a teacher. What kind of testimony would my life offer to past, present, and future students? I finally had to acknowledge that my actions inside and outside the classroom are all part of my legacy. *Who* I am is just as significant as *what* I teach.

Each of us forms a legacy that influences upcoming generations. When we gratefully give our time, talent, or money to worthy causes, we become caretakers of God's own generosity. Sometimes we will be taken advantage of by recipients, but this risk is hardly a reason to refrain from bigheartedness. My student was a generous witness at the house-library. Even though he had little money to offer, he mirrored the love of Jesus Christ to the children. Perhaps one of the blessed kids will one day befriend other children even at the same library, perpetuating the neighborhood legacy.

Reflecting the Face of Christ

Ultimately each of our lives is a message that reflects what we love. Other people observe why and how we care. In biblical terms, we offer a "face" to others, a personal reflection of what is in our hearts. For a Christian, "facing reality" means seeing ourselves in the light of God's majesty, letting ourselves be illumined by his grace and truth. We are called to reflect the face of Christ, not merely our own countenance.

Jesus is our supreme example. He goes up a mountain to pray. There three followers see Jesus's face shining like the sun. Soon Moses and Elijah appear and talk with Jesus. Finally, a voice from a cloud says, "This is my Son, whom I love; with him I am well pleased. Listen to him!" The followers fall to the ground terrified.[11] Jesus's transformed appearance tells the followers that their rabbi was indeed the Christ, the Son of God.

Our faces reflect our values and commitments. Others—including God—see what makes us smile in gratitude or sneer in disgust. Jesus criticizes hypocritical religious leaders for shutting doors to the kingdom of heaven in people's faces—refusing to accept them as distinct persons worthy of reflecting God's grace.[12] Mockers spit in Jesus's face, as if to say that he was a despicable fraud.[13] Faithful people often fall facedown in reverential awe before Jesus's face—the same event that will occur upon Christ's return.[14]

Many professional persuaders recognize our human tendency to "put on" the faces of those we admire. Retailers display facial posters in mall storefronts in order to gain shoppers' attention. Graphic artists depict beautiful faces in magazine advertisements, on TV, and via billboards. Celebrity promoters peddle their clients' faces while the paparazzi capture candid shots of high-profile personalities.

In the midst of this facial bombardment, we are called to come face-to-face with Jesus Christ. God invites us to be intimate with the person of Jesus, to know the Lord so well that we mirror Jesus's heart and mind to others. Paul even says that our "unveiled faces" will reflect the Lord's glory as we are transformed into Christ's likeness.[15]

In other words, we should journey toward Jesus and become more like the Suffering Servant, thereby revealing the glory of God to others. Although we cannot be faultless mirrors of Christ, we can by grace reflect some of God's sacrificial care to the chaotic world.

Facial communication is an amazing aspect of our createdness. Researchers have discovered that a newborn child soon starts looking at nearby faces. Most incredibly, the distance between the eyes of a nursing child and the gaze of its mother is nearly perfect for the infant to begin focusing on the face of her or his life-sustainer. Then the child starts imitating more distant faces. So begins a lifetime of mirroring others' countenances.

We are born imitators. For good and for evil, we mimic other individuals and adopt their values and practices. This innate capacity is *mimetic desire—the human craving to imitate others*.

James addresses the role of mimetic desire in legacy. He describes a man who peers into a mirror, presumably because he wants to remind himself who he is. Then the man glances elsewhere and immediately forgets what he saw in the mirror.[16] His own face makes no lasting impression on him!

This forgetful man has a physical face, but he has no lasting self-identity in Christ. He doesn't really know that he is a child of God. In order to discover himself, he will have to look longer, deeper, beyond the superficial image of himself. In fact, he will have to peer into God's Word in order to capture most completely the "image" of Christ.

We discover our true selves in our relationship with Jesus Christ. The more intimate we become with the Son of God, the more fully we will recognize that we are made in the image and likeness of a caring God. Our legacy then can reflect God's glory rather than our own flesh in a mirror. Without Christ, our faces become undistinguished expressions of socially constructed personae. Too often even followers of Jesus follow music stars, models, and Hollywood personalities rather than saintly followers who humbly look up to the Lord.

This is why Christian artists historically painted righteous believers who were facing the resurrected Lord. As depicted on canvas, such followers mirrored God's truth and goodness. Moreover, artists sometimes depicted believers looking at saints, who were themselves peering at Christ. The point of such glimpses of the faces of faithful believers was to direct others to the person of Jesus.

All followers of Jesus Christ are called to form holy, humble legacies that reflect the love of God. In order to do this, we imitate Christ as he is described in the Scriptures. Paul writes that we now see only a poor reflection in a mirror. Eventually we will see the living God face-to-face. We will then know God the way that Jesus now knows us.[17]

Conclusion

Our legacy becomes our lasting witness to others. Most people begin to understand the call to legacy when they have children. A colleague who had nine offspring told me that God gives children in order to discipline the parents. I thought he was exaggerating until I had children and witnessed them imitating my wife and me. We realized that we had better live as worthy, even though imperfect, role models.

During high school, college, and then again at midlife, followers often ask serious questions about how they want to spend their remaining time on earth. They wonder how to give back to God in gratitude for all that they have received.

Just before Grandpa John died, he was ready to complete his journey on earth by meeting Jesus face-to-face. He had spent more than a century being as faithful a follower as he could by the grace of God. Sure, he was like all of us, a sinner with regrets. And his body was weakening, his memory was fading, and his mind was playing tricks on him. Grandpa John's emotional highs and lows as well as his deteriorating body and mind were sad to witness.

Yet he still broke out in song, suddenly praising the Lord as he had done since he was a boy. His favorite hymn, "Great Is Thy Faithfulness," helped us to remember God's goodness throughout this caretaker's faithful journey. In the face of one saintly man, we caught a glimpse of the glory of a caring God. The most fitting response to our memories of Grandpa John, as long as they last, is to love God by offering our own lives as living sacrifices.

Our highest calling is to follow Jesus Christ, the great caretaker of his sheep. When we embark on this mysterious adventure, opening our hearts to God, we are in for many surprises. Perhaps most astonishing of all, when we care in his name, we discover that he has been there before us, preparing the way. We are able to care because Christ first cared skillfully for and compassionately about us. God's own legacy precedes us in creation, in the Scriptures, and in the work of the Spirit among us. Yet in his glorious mercy, Jesus Christ prepares stations for us so that we can participate humbly in his renewal of all things in heaven and on earth.

Suggested Reading

Chapter 1: Listening to God

John Milton's quote is from Sonnet 19. The distinction between vocation and station often is attributed to Martin Luther (1483–1546), but it has long been part of the church's understanding of faithfulness. See Luther's *The Freedom of a Christian*. Various Christian perspectives on vocation are covered in Lee Hardy, *The Fabric of This World: Inquiries into Calling, Career Choice, and the Design of Human Work* (Grand Rapids: Eerdmans, 1990). John Calvin (1509–1564) said that God gives us particular "sentry posts" so we don't wander carelessly through life (*Institutes of the Christian Religion*, 3·10.6). Another way of defining "station" is the "range of our effective will." See Dallas Willard, *The Divine Conspiracy: Rediscovering Our Hidden Life in God* (San Francisco: HarperSanFrancisco, 1998), 21. Martin Luther King Jr.'s weaknesses and strengths are discussed in Michael Eric Dyson, *I May Not Get There with You: The True Martin Luther King Jr.* (New York: The Free Press, 2000). A brief review of Augustine's life is Garry Wills, *Saint Augustine* (New York: Viking, 1999). Anne Lamott's prayers are from *Traveling Mercies: Some Thoughts on Faith* (New York: Pantheon, 1999), 82. The idea of discovering God's will for one's life is complex and worthy of much more comment. Among the books that question our ability to know God's specific will for stations is Bruce K.

Waltke, *Finding the Will of God: A Pagan Notion?* (Grand Rapids: Eerdmans, 2002).

Chapter 2: Participating in Renewal

Richard J. Mouw discusses Isaiah 60 and the renewal of heaven and earth in *When the Kings Come Marching In: Isaiah and the New Jerusalem*, revised edition (Grand Rapids: Eerdmans, 2002). Augustine's notion of using one's entire body as an alleluia to God is from Saint Augustin [*sic*], *Expositions on the Book of the Psalms*, trans. and ed. Philip Schaff, A Select Library of the Nicene and Post-Nicene Fathers of the Christian Church, Vol. 8 (Grand Rapids: Eerdmans, 1956), 673–74. For a biblical look at how God takes up residence in our weaknesses, see Marva Dawn, *Powers, Weakness, and the Tabernacling of God* (Grand Rapids: Eerdmans, 2001). St. Francis of Assisi's recommendation for friars comes from chapter XVII of his Rule of 1221. Mother Teresa's struggles are discussed in Carol Zaleski, "The Dark Night of Mother Teresa," *First Things*, May 2003, 24–27. The last stanza of "O for a Thousand Tongues to Sing" is quoted from the *Psalter Hymnal* (Board of Publications of the Christian Reformed Church, Grand Rapids, 1976).

Chapter 3: Succeeding Wholeheartedly

Henri J. M. Nouwen's quote is from his *The Way of the Heart* (New York: Ballantine, 1981), 9. A wonderful book on the importance of the heart in Christian theology and biblical interpretation is James M. Houston, *The Heart's Desire: Satisfying the Hunger of the Soul* (Vancouver: Regent College, 2001). Blaise Pascal (1623–1662) was a fine Christian writer on matters of the heart. A good introduction to his work is Thomas V. Morris, *Making Sense of It All: Pascal and the Meaning of Life* (Grand Rapids: Eerdmans, 1992), especially chapter 10. Madeleine L'Engle discusses artistry and sacrifice in *Walking on Water: Reflections on Faith and Art* (Wheaton: Harold Shaw, 1980), 223–24. The idea that human victory is based on dying with the most toys is from Catherine M. Wallace, *Selling Ourselves Short: Why We*

Struggle to Earn a Living and Have a Life (Grand Rapids: Brazos, 2003), 15. A moving book on suffering for Christ is Kay Marshall Strom and Michele Rickett, *Daughters of Hope: Stories of Witness and Courage in the Face of Persecution* (Downers Grove, IL: InterVarsity, 2003).

Chapter 4: Caring Responsibly

William Rodriguez's story is reviewed in Jane Ammeson, "Peace on Turf," *World Traveler*, December 1997, 53. Cornelius Plantinga Jr.'s discussion of vocation as prime citizenship is from *Engaging God's World* (Grand Rapids: Eerdmans, 2002), 110. The idea of renewing "every square inch" of God's creation is from Abraham Kuyper, *Lectures on Calvinism* (Grand Rapids: Eerdmans, 1931), 27. Martin Luther King Jr.'s story is from *Strength to Love* (New York: Pocket Books, 1963), 92–93. John Calvin discusses the human calling to be "stewards of everything" in book 3, chapter 7, section 5 of his *Institutes*. Simone Weil's quote is from *Waiting for God* (New York: G.P. Putnam's Sons, 1951), 64. The story of the skilled physician who cares for his patients, not just their organs, is in Thomas K. Arnold, "Dr. Theodore Ganiats," *San Diego Magazine*, October 2003, 68. Compassion is discussed in Donald P. McNeil, Douglas A. Morrison, and Henri J. M. Nouwen, *Compassion: A Reflection on the Christian Life* (Garden City, NY: Doubleday, 1982); and Bill Hybels, *Making Life Work: Putting God's Wisdom into Action* (Downers Grove, IL: InterVarsity, 1998), chapter 10. Ernest Gordon's story is from his autobiography about life in Japanese prison camps, *Miracle on the River Kwai* (London: Collins, 1965), 107–8. Gordon's book has since been republished as *To End All Wars* (Grand Rapids: Zondervan, 2002).

Chapter 5: Celebrating Leisure

The monastic notion of speaking only to improve upon the silence is from Anthony de Mello, *Taking Flight* (New York: Doubleday Image Books, 1988), 27. Also see the Rule of St. Benedict in any of its published forms. For background on contemplation, see Josef Pieper, *Happiness & Contemplation*, trans. Richard and Clara Winston (South Bend, IN: St. Augustine's Press, 1998). A Christian introduction to leisure is Josef Pieper, *Leisure: The Basis of Culture*, trans. Gerald Malsbary (South Bend, IN: St. Augustine's Press, 1998). A fine summary of Sabbath keeping is Marva J. Dawn, *Keeping the Sabbath Wholly: Ceasing, Resting, Embracing, Feasting* (Grand Rapids: Eerdmans, 1989). Also see Dorothy C. Bass, *Receiving the Day: Christian Practices for the Opening of the Gift of Time* (San Francisco: Jossey-Bass, 2000). Three books that I have found particularly helpful for understanding worship are: John D. Witvliet, *Worship Seeking Understanding: Windows into Christian Practice* (Grand Rapids: Baker Academic, 2003); Marva J. Dawn, *A Royal "Waste" of Time: The Splendor of Worshiping God and Being Church for the World* (Grand Rapids: Eerdmans, 1999); and William H. Willimon, *Word, Water, Wine and Bread: How Worship Has Changed over the Years* (Valley Forge, PA: Judson, 1980). C. S. Lewis's essay is "Petitionary Prayer: A Problem without an Answer," in *C. S. Lewis Essay Collection: Faith, Christianity and the Church*, ed. Lesley Walmsley (London: HarperCollins, 2000), 197–205. Also see N. T. Wright, *The Lord & His Prayer* (Grand Rapids: Eerdmans, 1996). Living prayerfully, or "friendship with Christ," is addressed in James Houston, *The Transforming Power of Prayer: Deepening Your Friendship with God* (Colorado Springs: NavPress, 1996).

Chapter 6: Flourishing in Communities

Dietrich Bonhoeffer's quotes are from *Life Together*, trans. John W. Doberstein (New York: Harper & Row, 1954), introduction and p. 17. The biblical concept of "shalom" is discussed in Nicholas Wolterstorff, *Until Justice and Peace Embrace* (Grand Rapids: Eerdmans, 1983), 69–72. St. Augustine of Hippo addressed community-based interpretation of Scripture in many writings, but essential is *De Doctrina Christiana*. I summarize his thoughts in Quentin J. Schultze, *Communicating for Life: Christian Stewardship in Community and Media* (Grand Rapids: Baker, 2000), chapter 4. Cornelius Plantinga Jr.'s ideas on professions as agents of social renewal are in *Engaging God's World*, 122. Frederick Buechner's concept of vocation as serving "hungry" people with gladness is from *Wishful Thinking: A Seeker's ABC* (San Francisco: HarperSanFrancisco, 1993), 119. Eugene H. Peterson's quote about professional exploitation is from *Where Your Treasure Is: Psalms that Summon You from Self to Community* (Grand Rapids: Eerdmans, 1993), 7. One perspective on the importance of singlehood in the biblical tradition is Rodney Clapp, *Families at the Crossroads: Beyond Traditional & Modern Options* (Downers Grove, IL: InterVarsity, 1993), chapter 5. Billy Graham mentioned his regrets about not spending more time with his family during a speech in Grand Rapids, Michigan, in 1999. See Charley Honey, "Listening Heralds Dawn of New Age," *Grand Rapids Press*, 30 October 1999, B1.

Chapter 7: Loving for Good

Sources on hospitality include: Thomas W. Ogletree, *Hospitality to the Stranger: Dimensions of Moral Understanding* (Philadelphia: Fortress, 1985); Christine D. Pohl, *Making Room: Recovering Hospitality as a Christian Tradition* (Grand Rapids: Eerdmans, 1999); Michele Hershberger, *A Christian View of Hospitality: Expecting Surprises* (Scottdale, PA: Herald Press, 1999); and Lucien Richard, O.M.I., *Living the Hospitality of God* (New York: Paulist Press, 1989). The John Perkins and Thomas Tarrant book is *He's My Brother: Former Racial Foes Give a Strategy for Reconciliation* (Grand Rapids: Baker, 1994). Books on friendship include: Isabel Anders, *Faces of Friendship* (Cambridge, MA: Cowley, 1982); and John W. Crossin, *Friendship: The Key to Spiritual Growth* (New York: Paulist Press, 1997).

Chapter 8: Offering a Legacy

Living gratefully is discussed in: David Steindl-Rast, *Gratefulness: The Heart of Prayer* (New York: Paulist Press, 1990); and William H. Willimon, *The Service of God: How Worship and Ethics are Related* (Nashville: Abingdon, 1983), 194–99. A fine introduction to mimetic desire is René Girard, *I See Satan Fall Like Lightning* (New York: Orbis, 2001). One of the most interesting and accessible examinations of the visual portrayal of

Jesus's face throughout history is Jaroslav Pelikan, *Jesus through the Centuries: His Place in the History of Culture* (New Haven: Yale University Press, 1985). Also see N. T. Wright, *For All God's Worth: True Worship and the Calling of the Church* (Grand Rapids: Eerdmans, 1997), chapter 6.

Notes

Introduction

1. Phil. 2:12–13

Chapter 1

1. Heb. 11:11
2. Ps. 139:16
3. Eph. 1:11
4. Acts 9
5. Lev. 19:18; Matt. 22:37–40; James 2:8
6. Phil. 2:12
7. See, e.g., 2 Chron. 23:19; Neh. 4:13
8. Luke 1:38
9. Gen. 22:1
10. Ps. 8:5
11. Rom. 9:20–23

Chapter 2

1. Job 14:1; 42:2
2. Amos 9:1
3. Matt. 19:28
4. Eph. 2:10

5. Matt. 19:28; Eph. 1:10
6. Matt. 18:22
7. Micah 6:8
8. Eph. 1:10
9. Rev. 21:1–2
10. 1 Cor. 15:58; 2 Peter 3:13
11. Gal. 4:14
12. Eph. 1:19
13. Heb. 11:37–38
14. 2 Sam. 11
15. Exod. 4:10
16. Exod. 6:9
17. Exod. 6:12
18. Exod. 7:1–5
19. Matt. 26:34
20. Acts 4:13
21. Heb. 11:8
22. Heb. 11:12

Chapter 3

1. Luke 12:34; Rom. 10:10
2. Ps. 19:14

3. Pss. 11:2; 13:2; 5:9; 15:2; 17:3; 19:14; 16:9; 28:7; 37:31; 119:2
4. Rom. 12
5. Phil. 2:12
6. Luke 10:25–28
7. John 17
8. 1 Cor. 10:17
9. Phil. 2:3–4
10. Phil. 2:7–9
11. Matt. 6
12. 1 Tim. 6:10
13. Matt. 6:21
14. Matt. 19:16–22
15. Matt. 5:3
16. Rom. 8:17
17. Phil. 4:11
18. Matt. 16:26; Luke 9:25
19. Matt. 6:33

Chapter 4

1. Luke 10:25–37
2. Gen. 2:15; Josh. 23:6, 11; Ps. 8:4; John 21:16
3. 1 Cor. 3:21
4. Col. 1:20; Eph. 1:10
5. Luke 16:2
6. 1 Cor. 12:31
7. Phil. 4:8
8. Col. 3:12
9. Gal. 5:22–23
10. Phil. 4:9
11. Matt. 25:14–30
12. Matt. 25:29

Chapter 5

1. Isa. 44:23; 55:12
2. Luke 14:5
3. Matt. 11:28–30
4. Gen. 1:31
5. Exod. 20

6. Heb. 4:3, 10
7. Luke 13:16
8. Heb. 13:5; Deut. 31:6
9. Ps. 95:6
10. 1 Cor. 14:26
11. 1 Tim. 2:1
12. Rom. 12:1
13. Eph. 5:25–27
14. 1 Thess. 5:17; Eph. 6:18; Luke 18:1; 21:36
15. Ps. 34:1
16. Matt. 21:22
17. 1 Thess. 5:16–19

Chapter 6

1. 1 Cor. 2:16
2. Gen. 1:2
3. Gen. 1:31
4. 1 Cor. 2:16
5. Rom. 10:9
6. Rom. 13:9; Gal. 5:14
7. Heb. 7:24
8. Rom. 15:30
9. Ps. 52:8

Chapter 7

1. John 15:12–13
2. See, e.g., Matt. 27:7; Eph. 2:12 regarding the "foreigner."
3. Rom. 12:13
4. Rom. 12:9–13
5. Matt. 25:37–40
6. Gen. 18
7. Luke 14:12–14
8. Matt. 25:34–46; Heb. 13:2
9. 2 Cor. 4:6
10. Mark 12:31
11. Mark 12:33
12. Rev. 7:9

13. 1 John 4:7
14. 1 Cor. 12:7

Chapter 8
1. Matt. 7:3; Rom. 1:21
2. Rom. 8:28
3. Jer. 31:29
4. Heb. 8:12
5. Heb. 12:1
6. 1 Tim. 6:18
7. James 1:5
8. Luke 10:38–42
9. Prov. 11:25
10. 2 Cor. 9:6
11. Matt. 17:1–6
12. Matt. 23:13
13. Matt. 26:67
14. Rev. 7:11
15. 2 Cor. 3:18
16. James 1:23–24
17. 1 Cor. 13:12

Quentin J. Schultze (Ph.D., University of Illinois) is a nationally known communication expert whose many books include *Habits of the High-Tech Heart* and *High-Tech Worship?* He is the Arthur H. DeKruyter Chair in Faith & Communication and director of the Gainey Institute for Faith & Communication at Calvin College.

Also available from
Quentin J. Schultze . . .

What is a **theology** of **communication**?

What is the relationship between **communication**, **community**, and **communion**?

Examine how your communication affects community and how the media in your life—whether oral, written, electronic, or digital communication—influence you spiritually.

AVAILABLE WHEREVER CHRISTIAN BOOKS ARE SOLD.